LIBERAL PURITANISM

'GOD AND LIFE' SERIES

Edited by B. AQUILA BARBER

A PORTRAIT OF PAUL.
J. ALEXANDER FINDLAY, M.A., D.D.

LIBERAL PURITANISM.
A. W. HARRISON, M.C., B.A., B.Sc., D.D.

IN PREPARATION

THE MESSAGE OF THE PARABLES.
R. E. ROBERTS, D.D.

INTERPRETERS OF LIFE.
ROBERT STRONG, M.A., B.Litt.

WHAT I BELIEVE.
A Symposium by Eminent Ministers and
Laymen, with an Introduction by the Editor.

THE HEAVENLY OCTAVE: A STUDY
OF THE BEATITUDES.
FRANK W. BOREHAM, D.D.

METHODIST GOOD COMPANIONS.
G. ELSIE HARRISON, B.A.

HAVE FAITH IN GOD.
NORMAN H. SNAITH, M.A. (Oxon.).
Senior Kennicott Hebrew Scholar, 1925.

LIBERAL PURITANISM

By

A. W. HARRISON

M.C., B.A., B.Sc., D.D.

Author of

Christianity and the League of Nations,
Christianity and Universal Peace,
All that Jesus Began,
The Beginnings of Arminianism, &c.

LONDON

THE EPWORTH PRESS

(EDGAR C. BARTON)

25-35 CITY ROAD, E.C. 1

First Edition, 1935

Made and Printed in Great Britain by
RICHARD CLAY AND SONS, LTD.
BUNGAY, SUFFOLK

CONTENTS

PREFACE

The following essays (with the exception of that on 'Liberal Puritanism') have appeared in the *Hibbert Journal*, the *London Quarterly Review* and the *Holborn Review*. That on 'Oliver Cromwell' appeared in the January 1935 issue of the *London Quarterly and Holborn Review* under the title, 'The Constable of England.' I wish to express my thanks to the publishers of these two reviews (now fused into one) for their permission to reprint six essays (including one on the Lollards by my wife). I am also grateful to the Editor of the *Hibbert Journal* for allowing me to add to this volume the essays on 'Romanticism in Religious Revivals' and on 'The Philosophy of D. H. Lawrence,' which appeared in July 1933 and July 1934, respectively.

A. W. HARRISON.

Westminster College,
London,
February, 1935.

I

LIBERAL PURITANISM

PURITANISM has come in these days (I know not how) to
be considered as much a subject for contempt as it was in
the days of the Restoration. Charles II is said to be a
more attractive theme than Cromwell, even in the depleted
ranks of our present-day Liberals in the House of Commons.
It may be that they represent a degenerate Liberalism; one
hesitates to believe that Restoration morals and Restoration
cynicism are characteristics of our own age. The English
Puritans eventually developed into the party that challenged
the autocracy of absolute rule in Church and State.
It would have set the tenure, not only of kings and
magistrates, but of bishops and priests in the will of
the people. It created modern democratic government;
though by an accident it came into power for a few years
itself as an autocracy. In its historic period it gave us in
Cromwell the greatest of our men of action, in Milton the
most exalted of our poets, and in Bunyan the most widely-
read writer that England ever produced. These seem
inadequate reasons for the contemptuous abuse of Puritans
so common to-day. We can understand why Butler's
Hudibras was so popular when it first appeared. A cari-
cature of the extreme forms of fanaticism that showed
themselves under the Commonwealth was delightful to
Cavaliers who had suffered so many defeats at their hands.
Hudibras is not read to-day, but a few phrases stick in the
mind. Even Pepys could get very little amusement out of

it and was glad to sell his half-crown copy for eighteenpence, after being bored by the silly abuse of the Presbyter Knight going to the wars. But Pepys was enough of a realist to see that the Restoration was not all gain. As early as 1667 we find him reporting that ' it is strange how every-body do now-a-days reflect upon Oliver, and commend him, what brave things he did, and made all the neighbour princes fear him; while here a prince come in with all the love and prayers and good liking of his people, who have given greater signs of loyalty and willingness to serve him with their estates than ever was done by any people, hath lost all so soon that it is a miracle what way a man could devise to lose so much in so little time.'

Charles II was an amusing and good-tempered monarch, with much more ability and capacity for work than appears at first sight, but his present-day apologists should put that sentence of Pepys down and remember that it needs explanation. Puritanism in 1667 had degenerated into a defeated and dying Nonconformity. If it were in its essence merely what Butler represents it to be in his Pindaric ode *Upon a Hypocritical Nonconformist*, it would be a waste of time to try to defend it. Why should we try to defend hypocrisy, dogmatic ignorance, censoriousness and truculent cantankerousness ? But Puritanism, in the narrow English meaning of the term, stood for something better than that. There had been days, thirty or forty years earlier, when Puritanism stood for half the nation, and for what appeared to be the better half. James I lived long enough to find out that the best laymen in the Established Church were Puritans, and his son succeeded in uniting the Commons against himself until they split asunder over the Root and Branch reform of the Church. Even then 700 or 800 of the clergy were opposed to the growth of ceremonies in the Church and in favour of reform, though not necessarily of the suppression, of episcopacy. The name of Puritan dated as far back as 1570 and stood for those who desired 'a purer Reformation.' They desired 'even the reforming of Reformation itself.' It was a plea for the simplicity of the primitive Church, for purity in morals and for righteousness in the national life as well as in that of the individual. It derived from a Calvinistic theology in which righteousness was the chief attribute of the Almighty. The God of the earlier Puritans was not the source of joy and beauty and intellectual eminence. This was the weak side of their teaching, but in righteousness was their strength. The new translations of the Bible became the vehicle of their thought; the very words of Scripture were constantly upon their lips, the natural expression of what was deepest in their view of life. In the fellowship of the prophets they entered into immediate fellowship with the Eternal Spirit, and the significance of rites and ceremonies became merely secondary. There were many men of culture like-minded with Colonel Hutchinson, who 'hated outsides in religion.'

It is clear that such an attitude has its perils. Intensity of belief soon becomes intolerant. It may become fanatical and extravagant. Is it possible to speak of a Liberal Puritanism ? One of the fundamental principles of Liberalism is toleration. It stands for liberty of thought, liberty of speech, liberty of action in so far as these are possible without destroying the Commonwealth. It has been said that 'a Liberal may be defined approximately as a man who, if he could by waving his hand in a dark room, stop the mouths of all the deceivers of mankind for ever, would not wave his hand.' The Puritan could not rise to that high level of toleration. Indeed, Cromwell, as the Puritan autocrat, seems the very antithesis of Liberalism. Yet few men in the seventeenth century, raised to such a dangerous eminence, would have shown such a spirit of toleration. Religious toleration as a principle of State Government came from the Puritans. They may have learned it in the school of adversity, but the liberties granted to Rhode Island by Roger Williams and regarded as eccentric in the seventeenth century, became the commonplaces of the nineteenth century. We have lived to see the twentieth century return to a view of the State as the power that regulates the opinions as well as the actions of its subjects. The cause of liberty can best be served in our day by a new race of Puritans whose faith in God is only equalled by their love for man; who have so learned the best in liberal theology as well as liberal politics that they believe in a God who is the source of beauty, truth and love as well as righteousness, and find that the simplicity of the Gospel does not quarrel about rites and Church organization, but serves humanity in the spirit of its Master and Lord. If the God of Puritanism may be a God who does not

> Send ane to heaven and ten to hell
> A' for Thy glory,

but rejoices in the beauty of sun and sea and pleasant landscape, in the love of men and women, in the laughter of little children and in all innocent and pleasing joys then a Liberal Puritanism is a possibility; nay, it may be the greatest of boons to mankind.

The chief cause of the unpopularity of Puritanism may be found in its reputed hostility to popular amusements. The famous phrase of Macaulay that 'the Puritan hated bear-baiting, not because it gave pain to the bear, but because it gave pleasure to the spectators' is the kind of calumny that has the secret of perpetual life. It is an amusing travesty of an attitude that was certainly rigid, but with just reason. If bear-baiting and cock-fighting have been suppressed as public entertainments in England, the Puritan deserves some praise for that suppression. Mr. Percy Scholes, in his recently published and very learned book on *The Puritans and Music*, does not hesitate to say of a long passage on Puritanism quoted from Macaulay's well-known first chapter that it is 'false from beginning to end.' It is true that the play-houses were closed under the Commonwealth, but Mr. Scholes says, in reply to a reviewer of his book who had spoken of 'the cessation of public entertainments under the Protectorate,' 'this is just the kind of phrase which, written doubtless with a restricted meaning, is necessarily read with a more comprehensive one. Can we talk of a "cessation of public entertainments" when masques continued and opera began, when puppet-plays went on (with all the rest of the fun of the fair —tight-rope walking, "monsters" &c.), when dancing-schools were freely open, when Cromwell, on occasion, allowed horse-racing, when organ-recitals were given in the taverns and our English concert system thus came into existence? Only one public entertainment was stopped —that of the spoken play. And that on grounds that are most strongly stated in the works not of Puritans, but of pre-Commonwealth Episcopalians like Stubbes. It is the unconsidered use by historian after historian of such expressions as "the cessation of public entertainments under the Protectorate" that has led to such a complete misconception as to the Puritan attitude to the pleasures of life.'

In his book Mr. Scholes not only shows the absurdity of the charge that the Puritans were opposed to music, but he proves that they were 'in the affairs of everyday life, perfectly normal citizens—like you and me.' He quotes passage after passage of misrepresentation from modern literature and traces these libels to their source, but however

completely these charges may be rebuked the adjective
'puritanical' will remain an abusive epithet.   The Puritans
are not to be forgiven for closing the theatres.   They did
not object to the play as such, but they did object to the
immorality and indecency that had come to be associated
with the play-house.   If Episcopalians like Stubbes held
the same views in pre-Commonwealth days, equally good
Anglicans restated them when they were outraged by the
Restoration stage.   It is not Milton but Evelyn who says
(Oct. 18, 1666), ' This night was acted my Lord Broghill's
tragedy, called Mustapha, before their Majesties at Court,
at which I was present; very seldom going to the public
theatres for many reasons now, as they were abused to an
atheistical liberty; foul and indecent women now (and
never till now) permitted to appear and act, who inflaming
several young noblemen and gallants, became their misses,
and to some, their wives.   Witness the Earl of Oxford,
Sir R. Howard, Prince Rupert, the Earl of Dorset, and
another greater person than any of them, who fell into their
snares, to the reproach of their noble families, and ruin of
both body and soul.'   It remained for Jeremy Collier, an
Anglican and not a Dissenting divine, to write the word
of condemnation on the stage of the Restoration at the
end of the century in his *Immorality and Profaneness of the
English Stage* (1698).   After that there was a change for the
better, and *The Spectator* must accept its share of responsibility for challenging public amusements that were offensive
to good taste if not to morality and religion.   Are we then
to group Addison and Steele with the Puritans ?

Of course there were extremists who went further.
Some were opposed to plays in themselves; some were
even opposed to the novel, as an abuse of truth.   I have
memories of such opponents of fiction who would denounce
a Dickens or a Thackeray as ' some lie or other.'   In-

hibitions that would not allow a Christian to play games, or to smoke, let alone be seen in theatres or music-halls, were common enough in certain circles. Perhaps Victorian Nonconformity had more than its fair share of such people, but a Roman Catholic peasant held very similar views. Indeed, it may be argued that Roman Catholicism can be more 'Puritan' than the Puritans themselves. In these present days it is the Roman Catholics in the United States who are leading the campaign against indecent and degrading films. They deserve every credit for it. In this country attempts to limit opportunities for drunkenness, for gambling, for dog-racing and for the more brutal type of prize-fight are denounced as Puritanical, and Nonconformity is often regarded as the present-day representative of a seventeenth-century party. The 'Nonconformist conscience' is not as troublesome as it was a generation ago, but its slumbers are fitful. At the present moment there is some discussion taking place about the increasing tendency to nudity on the stage. It is significant that it was started by a Bishop, but the Puritans are getting most of the abuse in the correspondence. Is it not true to say that Christianity, whenever it has been in earnest, has always objected to public displays that tend to rouse the lusts and passions of men? From Tertullian to the present day it would be easy to collect a long series of such objections, gathered from almost every school of Christian thought. In fact, Puritanism is not a seventeenth-century English phenomenon which has merely continued its influence among the English speaking peoples down to the present; it is a recurring phase in Christian history and may be found at every period of religious revival.

Puritanism may indeed be regarded as a sign of revival in religion by its very intensity. Revival has always come as the result of a strenuous endeavour to recover primitive

B

Christianity. When this attempt is made a certain ascetic
simplicity is the result. The ' good soldier of Jesus Christ '
submits to a rigid discipline. He is at war with worldliness
and he knows that if he takes his warfare seriously, he is
not permitted to compromise with the enemy. Conscience
is the rule of life. He walks as ' ever in the great Task-
master's eye.' His strictness is in danger of becoming
censorious and if he is sufficiently rigid in his attitude his
more tolerant comrades will begin to charge him with
heresy and sectarianism. Simplicity in worship will
naturally accompany his black and white view of mankind.
His enthusiasm will lead to reform not in the individual
alone, but in society. His indifference to worldly rank
and status will bring the common man into prominence.
He has a gospel that will ' enrich the humble poor.' The
less men are entangled in the complexities of civilization,
the more will a Puritanical simplicity appeal to them.
Occasionally that appeal will be made to the man who
is stifled by the trappings of life, but that is the exception
and not the rule. Monasticism is the extremest form of
Puritanism in its reaction against worldliness; the most
heroic attempt in history

> To tear deep-rooted passion from the heart
> To still the inward strife.

Puritanism in its widest sense is, therefore, woven into the
texture of Christian history. The mention of Tertullian as
a typical third-century Puritan leads us to consider Montanism as an early Puritan movement that has been much
misrepresented by orthodox Church historians. After the
repression of the Montanists the Puritan movement ran
in the narrow channels of Monasticism. That long story
would lead us too far afield, but we are on the main
highway again when we meet with St. Francis in his
endeavour to follow naked a naked Christ.

It may be a surprise to some to find Francis of Assisi
in this high fellowship. The gay and cheerful attitude of
the Friars (*ioculatores Domini*) is sometimes represented as
the very antithesis of Puritanism. If every Puritan were
' sour-faced ' there would be some point in such a contrast,
for we should never apply that adjective to Francis. Dr.
Coulton, in discussing ' the high ancestry of Puritanism '
and illustrating it from the Middle Ages, says of *The Little
Flowers of St. Francis*, ' that charming idyll no more
represents the real bitterness of the war against the world
in the thirteenth century than Lucy Hutchinson's memoirs
show us the bitterness of the seventeenth-century Leveller.'
The serious endeavour to follow Christ perfectly, the
unworldliness, the simplicity, the immediate experience of
religion that glow through the whole career of Francis find
many parallels among the Puritans. The closest parallel
to the preaching friars in later Church history is found in
the early Methodist preachers, who have the hall-marks
of Puritanism all over them. The Lollards have similar
characteristics, though they found themselves in sharp
antagonism to the degenerate friars of the latter part of
the fourteenth century. My wife's essay on ' The Lollards
in the Time of Richard II ' brings this out very clearly.
They had, however, this in common with the early Franciscans, that they were on the side of the people, *Fratres
Minores*, as much as the followers of Francis. If their
preaching was not directly political, we cannot entirely
dissociate the Peasants' Revolt from the religious teaching
of wandering preachers. The same phenomenon was seen
again in Germany at the Reformation. The greatest
tragedy in Luther's career was his savage reaction against
the ' murdering, thieving hordes of peasants.' It is not
fanciful to find a spiritual decline in the great Reformer
after his unfortunate outburst. The Lutheran Church

missed its great opportunity of becoming the Church of
the German people.   Critics of the Reformation, who are
very vocal in these days, persistently fail, however, to do
justice to Luther as one of the greatest spiritual influences
in Christian history.   It is in the sphere of Christian
experience, rather than in politics, that the Reformation was
born.   Luther did not search for the way of salvation with
impassioned intensity for twenty years in vain.

The Reformation theology that found its classical
expression in the *Institutes* of Calvin had too dark a view
of human nature.   Its stern doctrines of Predestination and
Reprobation coloured the whole Puritan view of life.   But
men were always better than their creed, and cheerfulness
would keep breaking through.   Milton and Cromwell will
find a place in any study of Puritanism, and the theology
of both lay under the shadow of Calvin.   The first
challenge to Calvinism within Protestantism came from
the Dutch divine Arminius.   His doctrines were held in
England in opposition to the Puritans by the High
Churchmen, but it was the Evangelical Revival that made
them popular.   In the Wesleys the Anglican and Puritan
traditions of the seventeenth century met and blended in a
remarkable way.   Their maternal and paternal grandfathers
as well as their great-grandfather on the father's side were all
Puritan Nonconformists who were expelled under the 1662
Act of Uniformity.   Their parents had returned to the Angli-
canism of the Caroline Divines.   Nevertheless, it was the
Puritan element that was the dominant one, and if we are surprised to find Romanticism in the poetry of Charles Wesley
and the experiences of the early Methodist preachers it is
because of a preconceived notion of the Puritan as a hard-
faced fanatic, a stranger to the joys of life.   R. L. Stevenson
finds himself in strange company here, but he never got away
from the Shorter Catechism, though he discovered a kindlier

humanism than Calvin ever knew.   D. H. Lawrence reacted
against the Puritanism of his youth and has been accepted
by a literary clique as the exponent of a new philosophy
now Christianity has come to be regarded 'among all
persons of discernment' (to quote Bishop Butler) 'as a
principal subject of mirth and ridicule, as it were by way
of reprisal, for its having so long interrupted the pleasures
of the world.'   D. H. Lawrence had a flame of genius and
was passionately sincere, but if his 'philosophy' is set
out in its crudest form it reveals the bankruptcy of such an
alternative to the restraint of Christian ethics.

These essays are merely indications of 'the high ancestry
of Puritanism.' The Hebrews are sometimes credited
with the origins of this great spiritual and moral influence
and, indeed, the Old Testament was a potent force in
seventeenth-century England. Neither the Hebrews nor
the English can claim a monopoly in Puritanism. Other
peoples produce their Savonarolas from time to time. In
the seventeenth century itself English Puritanism finds a
parallel in French Jansenism, though the national characteristics express themselves in different ways with widely
varying results even when moved by similar ideals. The
story of English Puritanism needs to be rewritten. While
the excesses of the extremists among the sectaries cannot be
ignored, the main current will be found in the lives of
country gentlemen and in the growing middle-class. The
story should begin with men like John Hampden and
Milton and Colonel Hutchinson rather than with the
Muggletonians. From the Reformation should be traced
the forces that made such strong personalities possible. A
generation of spiritual quickening lies behind them. The
Elizabethan mentality was aflame with intensity. The
greatest Puritans were no enemies of the intellect. 'Continental, if not English, critics,' said Professor Dowden,

' have recognized the fact that a Puritan strain has entered into much that is most characteristic of our literature.' Nor were the best Puritans hostile to the best elements in humane culture. Mrs. Hutchinson says of her husband, that he ' was apt for any bodily exercise; he could dance admirably well, but neither in youth nor riper years made any practice of it; he had skill in fencing such as became a gentleman; he had a great love of music, and often diverted himself with a viol, on which he played masterly; and he had an exact ear and judgement in other music; he had great judgement in paintings, graving, sculpture, and all liberal arts, and had many curiosities of value in all kinds; he took great delight in perspective glasses, and for his other rarities was not so much affected with the antiquity as with the merit of the work; he took much pleasure in improvement of grounds, in planting groves, and walks, and fruit trees, in opening springs and making fish-ponds; he was wonderfully neat, cleanly and genteel in his habit, and had a very good fancy in it, but he left off very early the wearing of anything that was costly, yet in his plainest negligent habit appeared very much a gentleman; . . . his conversation was very pleasant, for he was naturally cheerful, had a ready wit and apprehension; he was eager in everything he did, earnest in dispute, but withal very rational, so that he was seldom overcome; . . . there was a life of spirit and power in him that's not to be found in any copy drawn from him.'

The *Memoirs of the Life of Colonel Hutchinson* by his widow Lucy is one of the most delightful biographies in our language. It is a strange contrast as a picture of a Puritan to that of *Hudibras*. If Mrs. Hutchinson is charged with idolizing her husband and painting too flattering a likeness, it should be remembered that she, too, was a Puritan, and her own portrait comes out spontaneously as she writes.

The impartial reader will find himself in the presence of people with deep and sincere religious principles which have created a dignified and admirable quality of life. If they must be condemned because they suppressed unnecessary alehouses when they were in authority and would not allow publicans to brew any more if they suffered ' disorder or debauchery ' in their houses, and if they were ' a little severe against drunkenness,' they are condemned in good company. The Puritan does stand for sobriety, and is sometimes a little too keen in enforcing his standards on other people. Let him keep his religious convictions and his moral earnestness, let him develop the spirit of broad-minded charity, and he will again be the saviour of his country, as he has often been in other days. Since the seventeenth century onwards, Puritanism has been the steadiest and sanest force in the life of the English-speaking peoples all over the world. The Evangelical Revival stimulated Puritanism anew and created movements towards philanthropy, democratic independence of thought and action, social and civic righteousness, honesty in the civil service and integrity in the national character which are potent still. If at times an irritating tendency to self-righteousness has also appeared from the same source, we need not be unduly surprised, nor allow our irritation to condemn the source itself. That would indeed be to throw out the baby with the bath-water. It will be an ill day for the British Empire and for the United States of America when Puritanism disappears as a chief component in the life of both peoples.

II

MONTANISM:
AN EARLY PARALLEL WITH METHODISM

The remarkable growth of the Early Church was not the result of the labours of the Apostles alone. Obscure and long-forgotten men and women toiled and wept and prayed in building that holy temple. Even from the New Testament we may gain some idea of the number of irregular ministries which were at work, and post-apostolic literature gives us glimpses of vigorous missionary activities. The vivid and interesting sidelights on the Corinthian Church in the letters of Paul are indicative of much. In the spring-tide of new religious enthusiasm we look for striking manifestations of the presence of the Divine Spirit. That Spirit bestows its charisms with no grudging hand on all who are born of the Spirit. In a Church assembly every Christian has his contribution: one chants a psalm or early Christian hymn, another gives a message of instruction, another announces some divine revelation granted to him in vision or dream, another breaks out in a manifestation of the strange gift of tongues which is translated by the saint endowed with the charism of interpretation. Little wonder that the 'wise' Corinthians laid too much emphasis on this mysterious gift. Paul tells them that the highest charism bestowed by the Spirit is the gift of love; but if they long for spiritual gifts, let them seek that which most edifies the Church—the gift of prophecy.

The importance of the prophet in the early Christian community can hardly be exaggerated. ' God hath set some in the Church,' says Paul, ' first apostles, secondly prophets '; and as the apostles passed away it would seem that the prophets naturally stepped into their place. True, their position was unofficial and irregular but none the less influential. They were the direct descendants of the Jewish prophets, as irregular and as unofficial as they, yet at the same time no less powerful. Among Jewish Christians they were given official recognition from the beginning, and very speedily the function passed over to the Gentile Churches. The man of keen spiritual insight and magnetic speech always must have his place in the Church. Their deepest utterances passed from lip to lip as expressing the inmost experience of the redeemed community and as veritably inspired. We are probably right in attributing the utterances in the Pastoral Epistles [1] introduced by the five times recurring phrase πιστὸς ὁ λόγος to these anonymous popular preachers of the Early Church. The Church was built on the good foundation laid by Paul and the other apostles, but we must not overlook the part played in laying that foundation by men whose names no longer survive. Some we hear of in the New Testament record : Agabus, Barnabas, Symeon Niger, Lucius of Cyrene, Manaen, Judas, and Silas, and of women the four daughters of Philip. In the Apocalypse we have a typical example of the highest expression of Christian prophecy.

There appear to have been two descriptions of prophets, the one itinerant, the other stationary. The latter would for the most part remain at their own occupation and in their own community. When the ' word was on them to deliver ' it broke forth in impassioned and eloquent utterance. The former wandered from church to church

[1] 1 Tim. i. 15, iii. 1, iv. 9; 2 Tim. ii. 11; Titus iii. 8.

with messages of exhortation. The long-lost *Teaching of the Twelve Apostles*, discovered in 1873, edited in 1883, and probably written about the beginning of the second century of our era, gives us many interesting hints as to the condition of the sub-apostolic Church in a period of transition. Nothing is more significant than the authority and influence of the prophets : they are the 'high priests' of the Church. If one of them settles in a Christian community as a regular pastor, he is to receive the first fruits of wine-press and threshing-floor, of oxen and of sheep. Wandering prophets were, however, to be subjected to somewhat severe tests. A prophet must give no signs of self-indulgence or greed; he must order no meal for himself and must move on after two days at the most.

When one considers how faith was jostling faith in a clamorous march to Rome in that busy first century, we can well understand why it should be necessary to test the itinerant prophet. It was an age when new faiths pressing in from the Orient were proclaimed with missionary zeal by wandering preachers of every type. It would be strange if eclectic philosophers of the road should not appropriate Christianity as part of their stock-in-trade and attempt to impose themselves on unsuspecting churches. Peregrinus Proteus, who is represented as duping the Christians of the second century in this way in a celebrated satire of Lucian, probably stands as a sample of multitudes of other impostors.

Paul's test of a prophet seems to us very inadequate : 'Wherefore I give you to understand that no man speaking in the Spirit of God saith Jesus is anathema; and no man can say Jesus is Lord but in the Holy Spirit.' If we give it a broad interpretation, however, we see how far-reaching is the scope of its application. A recognition of the full and absolute Lordship of Christ is the surest proof of the sincerity of the prophet and the value of his message.

As the years of the second century glided by, signs of decreasing fervour within the Church were not wanting. The charisms of the early days were less frequently manifested. The enthusiastic missionary was more and more replaced by the settled teacher. The influence of the great catechetical school of Alexandria at the end of the second century should be contrasted with the authority of the prophets at the end of the first. Quiet philosophical discourses are best fitted to the needs of an age which is beginning to forget the inspired seer. The question was forcing itself upon the consideration of the Church, whether it should exist as a society of religious devotees or should respond, on the other hand, to a call to a world-wide mission with an effective entrance to Roman society. Was it to pass, in the words of Renan, ' de l'état d'une petite chapelle de visionnaires à l'état d'église ouverte à tous ? ' [1] The tendency to secularize the Church was everywhere visible. Zion was beginning to question the fact that her conflict with the Empire was to the death, and to secure herself against authority by legal and political forms. A lower moral standard and a growing spirit of worldliness were also manifest. Side by side with these changes in the temper of the Christians, there were changes in organization. The contact of Christianity with strange Eastern faiths had left her face to face with peculiar heretics who called themselves orthodox. To defend herself against these the Church had to strengthen the hands of the faithful. Moreover, the decline of the irregular prophet made some more regular and more official ministry necessary. What was lacking in spiritual force had to be made good in delegated authority. The practical efficiency of an organization which set one man prominently forward as the representative of the local Church of the orthodox against

[1] *Marc Aurèle*, p. 238.

heresy and against impostors elevated the head of local colleges of presbyters to the position of bishop. Gradually the functions of the early prophet were assigned to the local bishop.

Montanism appears to have been a reaction against all these tendencies, so far as we can arrive at its real significance. The qualifying phrase is added with good reason. In the writings of the Fathers we are not to expect a perfectly unbiased judgement of any sect condemned by the Church. Observations with regard to Montanism may easily be paralleled in rancour by anti-Methodist publications of the Church of England in the eighteenth century : in neither case, however, can we take the view gathered from such documents as an accurate portrayal of the ' enthusiasts ' concerned. Happily the Methodists still exist to defend themselves, and their early apologies remain. The Montanists, on the contrary, have long since been exterminated, and we possess no account of them from their own standpoint except such as we gather from the writings of Tertullian and the Acts of Perpetua and Felicitas. Harnack accuses Eusebius, the great Church historian of the fourth century, of suppressing much of the testimony of Apollinarius, though he terms him ' a powerful weapon and antagonist of the Montanists.' Eusebius quotes largely from other books, especially from a certain anonymous author, but avoids Apollinarius because he was too generous in his judgement of the ' heretics.' Selwyn, on the contrary, inclines to the view that the anonymous author in question really was Apollinarius, the mistake being due to a false reading : his position cannot be regarded, however, as proved. We may then easily see why it is difficult to get at the real facts of the situation.

The Montanist ' heresy ' seems to have originated in Phrygia somewhere near the middle of the second century.

A certain Montanus, reputed to have been a priest of
Cybele, began to prophesy at the village of Ardabau, pro-
claiming that the era of the Paraclete had dawned. We
naturally look for some nineteenth-century German critic
who will prove to us that Montanus never existed, and we
find him in the person of Schwegler. A mythical personage
was invented to explain the name of the ' heresy,' as in the
analogous case of Ebionitism and its postulated founder
Ebion. It is certainly true that the personality of Montanus
is very shadowy. The few details of his career that are
preserved to us are all disputed, and on good grounds. It
is denied that he was originally a pagan priest, that the
epithets applied to him by Jerome (' abscissus,' ' semi-vir ')
were true, that he became a priest and afterwards bishop of
a Christian community ; eventually he committed suicide.
For the sake of poetic justice every heretic should end his
days in that manner, but records of such deaths by the
defenders of the faith are to be received with suspicion.
Montanus was soon overshadowed in importance by two
prophetesses—Priscilla and Maximilla by name—who left
their husbands to join the movement. We can best account
for the obscurity of the founder of the sect by assuming
his early death.

As to the date of the beginning of the movement we again
find ourselves in difficulties. The date given by Eusebius
(*circ*. A.D. 172) has been the one which hitherto has met with
most approval. We are aware from other sources that in
A.D. 177 the influence of Montanism had stirred the whole
Church, and was felt at Rome and in the Churches of South
Gaul. This seems an incredibly short space of time in which
the movement could make itself felt. One other authority,
Epiphanius, has three references in his chapters on the
Phrygian ' heresy ' which suggest the dates A.D. 100, 135,
and 157 respectively. Chronology was not the strong point

of ancient historians. De Soyres, in his valuable essay on the subject, leans to a date about A.D. 130; and Selwyn is only representing the modern tendency to an early date when he suggests A.D. 140.

We can well understand why Phrygia should be the scene of a revival of prophetic phenomena. It was in the centre of one of the greatest strongholds of Christianity. The four daughters of Philip, prophetesses, had lived in the neighbouring city of Hierapolis, and many well-known Christian prophets had worked in the neighbourhood. The Phrygian people were rude and fanatical, and these characteristics were especially manifest in their own religion. The supposed excesses of Montanism have been put down to the same source. Renan emphasizes the rural character of the district. ' Presque partout ailleurs le christianisme fut une religion de grandes villes : ici comme dans le Syrie au delà du Jourdain ce fut une religion de bourgades et de campagnards.' [1] In such a district and among such a people what kind of manifestation of supernormal religious feeling are we to expect ? The description of the rise of the movement which Eusebius quotes from his anonymous authority is worth reproducing :

' At a village called Ardabau, first they say when Gratus was proconsul of Asia, a recent convert, Montanus by name, through his unquenchable desire for leadership gave the adversary opportunity against him. And he became beside himself, and, being suddenly in a frenzy and ecstasy, he raved and began to babble and utter strange things, prophesying in a manner contrary to the constant custom of the Church handed down by tradition from the beginning.'

[1] *Marc Aurèle*, p. 211.

We have here a revival of the heathen frenzies of the local religion—such was the former view of the case. It seems a more accurate description to call it an exaggerated account of a late manifestation of Christian prophecy.

Epiphanius condemns Montanus because he supposes the Paraclete to say through him : ' Behold, man is as a lyre, and I hover round him as a plectrum : the man sleeps, and I watch.' Yet that very simile is applied by Justin in the same period to the inspiration of the Christian prophet, and Athenagoras in A.D. 176 has the same view of the divine enlightenment. Epiphanius, however, from the standpoint of a late date only sees in such frenzies a sign of madness. ' Atque hæc ipsa verba " volo et percutio et vigilio et Dominus corda in stuporem vertit " furiosi hominis verba sunt.' The second century mind, on the contrary, regarded such a manifest possession as either divine or diabolical. In the case of Montanus it was in doubt, but the Church finally decided to regard the phenomenon as Satanic.

What appears to have been new in these oracles was the insistence on the fact that the era of the Paraclete had begun. The prophets took up the teaching of John's Gospel, and applied many sayings from the last discourses of our Lord to their own inspiration.[1] The sect of the Alogi rejected the Gospel of John, and denied the existence of all Christian prophecy in reply to these lofty claims. The Montanists said that the first era was one of Law, then followed that of Christ, and now the greatest day had dawned, the Age of the Paraclete. All the new and pressing problems of the period would be solved by the oracles of the Paraclete. To the apostles the gift of the Holy Spirit might have been granted at Pentecost, but the Paraclete was reserved for Phrygia and the second century. Cyril of Jerusalem even ventures to assert that Montanus claimed to be the Paraclete

[1] John xiv. 16–21, 23, 26, xv. 20–26, xvi. 7–15, 25 ; and Matt. xxiii. 34.

himself. This is hardly credible in view of the inspired utterance of Maximilla, ' Do not hear me, but rather hear Christ.'

It may be convenient to gather together here some of the accusations and insinuations of patristic literature which seem to represent the mud which is the recognized substitute for argument.   Maximilla is reputed to have terminated her life by suicide, as did Montanus.   Apollonius descends to the unworthy dodge of innuendo by rhetorical questions : ' Does a prophet dye his hair ?   Does a prophet stain his eyelids ?   Does a prophet delight in adornment ?   Does a prophet play with tables and dice ?   Does a prophet lend on usury ? '   Jerome, in a letter to one of his lady admirers, accuses the Montanists of following the doctrine of Sabellius and of keeping three Lents as though three Saviours had suffered.   Hippolytus says that they assented to the doctrine of the Noetians and affirmed that the Father Himself was Son.   Moreover, they committed the heinous crime of indulging in repasts of radishes.   Patristic wit gave them the nickname of Tascodrugitæ, because of an assumed habit of holding the hand to the nose while praying.   One section of them, the Artotyritæ, is said to have made offerings of cheese with the bread in the Eucharist; and in support of this a passage is quoted from the Visions of St. Perpetua : She found herself in a spacious garden in which sat a man with white hair, in the garb of a shepherd, milking his sheep. He gave her a morsel of cheese (casa buccella), upon which ' I received it with folded hands and ate it, and all the saints around exclaimed " Amen." '   This may very well be an allusion to the Agape rather than the Eucharist, and is in any case no very clear demonstration of a ritual eating of cheese.   Cyril of Jerusalem says they baptized into the name of the Father and the Son and Montanus and Priscilla. The same person accuses them of infanticide, and proclaims

to the world the fact that Montanus, that most miserable
of men, cut the throats of wretched little children and then
chopped them up into horrid food. It is only charitable to
remember that this was written in the fervour of his youth-
ful orthodoxy. The same excuse, however, can hardly be
made for Augustine, who, at a later date, describes in detail
how the infants were bled by being pricked with needles,
how the blood was mixed with flour, kneaded into cakes,
and so consumed. Alas! even revered Fathers of the
Church were sadly too attentive to gossip, especially to such
as tended to the glory of orthodoxy and the shame of the
adversary.

Can nothing be said on the other side? How are we to
explain the fact that Epiphanius, in spite of his bias, was
compelled to admit that the Montanists were completely
orthodox? It is certainly true that Montanism made rapid
progress in Asia, so much so that the Phrygian bishops
endeavoured to exorcise the devils in the Montanist
prophetesses but did not succeed. Cappadocia, Galatia,
Cilicia, Thrace, Constantinople, were the areas next infected.
In A.D. 177 the confessors of the Churches of Vienne and
Lyons in South Gaul—closely connected with Asia and
possibly evangelized thence—are found writing to the
influential bishop of Rome to plead for peace with the
'heretics.' He is moreover said to have acknowledged
the prophetic gifts of Montanus, Priscilla, and Maximilla,
and to have bestowed his peace on the Churches of Asia
and Phrygia. After that, at the instigation of Praxeas the
Patripassian, the Roman bishop withdrew his approval.
His very hesitation is indicative of much. And when we
consider, finally, that the great Church Father, Tertullian,
was a convert to this strange 'heresy,' we shall pause before
we blindly accept the words of Hippolytus when he tersely
sums up the case by saying that ' it can be briefly proved to

C

all that many of their books are silly and their attempts at reasoning weak.'

If we are to discover anywhere at all the real nature of their beliefs, it will be from the writings of Tertullian. It is a matter of great regret that his seven books on Ecstasy have been lost. The finder of so valuable a treasure would be an even greater public benefactor than he who brings to light the lost books of Euclid. Tertullian never claimed that divine revelations had been granted to him, but believed thoroughly that such manifestations were given to others. In such an attitude he may be compared to Edward Irving or, with regard to questions of the experience of entire sanctification or of abnormal spiritual phenomena, to John Wesley. He quotes the holy prophetess Priscilla as saying : ' Purity is harmonious, and they [*i.e.*, the pure] see visions, and turning their faces downwards they even hear manifest voices as salutary as they are secret.' He quotes, with evident reverence, the utterances of the prophets as the immediate words of the Paraclete. The great point which he emphasizes, however, is the need for increased purity of life and more rigorous discipline in the Church. The bishop of Rome granted a decree of indulgence to readmit adulterers to Communion on repentance : the Church, moreover, permitted second marriages. Against this the Montanists held that mortal sinners could never be readmitted, and that second marriages were sin. They extolled asceticism, insisting on a stricter discipline of fasting, and denounced worldliness in all its forms. Tertullian maintained that every gay form of life, and even the study of science and art and worldly education, was of the devil. Clearly, the Montanists were the Puritan section of the Christian community.

Their importance from the standpoint of Church organization is rather due to the fact that they opposed the new

powers of the bishops, and represented the days when the
irregular prophet was of more consequence than the clergy.
It was not that they were entirely free from sacerdotal ideas
of the ministry.   Tertullian himself says : 'The right of
giving baptism belongs to the chief priest, that is, the
bishop.'   That, however, was said before his 'perversion':
afterwards he sets over against this his belief in the universal
priesthood of believers, including women.   'Are not we
laymen also priests ? . . . where there is no bench of clergy
you present the eucharistic offerings and baptize and are
your own sole priest.'   In such assertions we discover the
democratic elements of a movement which set itself against
a growing officialism.   This is clearly seen when we find
Tertullian speaking sarcastically of the bishop of Rome as
'the bishop of bishops,' and setting aside his judgement in
favour of that of 'that Vicar of the Lord, the Holy Spirit.
He, the Paraclete, is the only prelate, because He alone
succeeds Christ.'   Tertullian never denied that the Church
had the power of forgiveness and had received from Peter
the right to bar and unbar the gate of heaven.   But that
gift is to the spiritual not the psychic Church.   'The
Church then will truly forgive sins, but it will be the
Church of the Spirit . . . not the Church which consists of
bishops.'   The enlightened, who have received the Paraclete, are the 'spiritual'; ordinary Christians are but
'natural.'   Paul had said, 'The natural man receiveth not
the things of the Spirit of God'; and on this passage the
Montanists based their claim to be a spiritual aristocracy.
One can imagine how bitterly this claim would be resented
by the 'psychic Christians,' and how natural it would be
to put the Montanist side by side with the Gnostic, who
made a claim of an aristocracy of knowledge.   A sug-
gestive comparison could be made between Marcion and
Tertullian, although the destructive criticism of the one was

far more dangerous to the Church than that of the other. Both were reformers of intense conviction, endeavouring to lead the Church in opposite directions. Both alike struck at the theory of finality, which was the basis of the new ecclesiastical organization, while representing the extremes of idealistic and realistic movements respectively. The Church objected to the claim to superior spiritual insight on the one hand, and to what appeared to be a mere rationalizing philosophy on the other.

Renan puts the fundamental question of Montanism in this way. Is there or is there not an intermediary between the faithful and their God, and Montanus says, ' No, without hesitation.' In the main therefore we seem to be right in regarding Montanism as a conservative reaction to a more primitive form of our faith. The general position may be summed up in the noble words of Tertullian : ' Dominus noster Christus veritatem se, non consuetudinem cognominavit.' ' Truth rather than tradition ' is a motto capable of being twisted to unworthy use, but nevertheless indicates what is best in Montanism.

A word should be said with regard to the position of women in the movement. Epiphanius says without hesitation : ' Among them women are bishops and presbyters.' It is probably on the strength of this statement that we have the assurance of Renan : ' This strange form of Christianity claimed for women the right of performing all the functions of the clergy.' Tertullian gives a flat denial to this, and says that women did not hold office and only prophesied to the elect few when the congregation had gone home. Renan seems to derive a measure of amusement from the prophetesses and their methods. The prophetesses received money, clothes, and valuable gifts in return for their revelations. In his hands the Montanist prophetesses become almost as Parisian as the Jesus of his imagination. He makes merry over some festival in which these holy schismatic maidens took a prominent part. 'Seven virgins, carrying torches and clothed in white, entered the church, uttering groans of penitence, shedding torrents of tears, and expressing in eloquent gestures the wretchedness of human life. Then in the midst of the people they were seized with ecstasy, and began to preach and prophesy and fall into fits.' Remembering that Renan uses his sources without much discrimination, we shall receive such descriptions, emanating from the orthodox, *cum grano salis.*

It is probably true, however, that Montanus sought to establish a rival organization to the Church in Asia : elsewhere the Montanists seem to have remained in the Church and received its *regula.* Pepuza, another Phrygian village, was the headquarters of the sect, and a patriarch seems to have been established there. The three grades of the Montanist ministry are said to have been patriarchs, stewards (cenonæ), and bishops. This new and undivided commonwealth looked for the establishment of the New Jerusalem at Pepuza. The prophetess Priscilla describes a vision in which Christ came to her in the form of a woman, and informed her that Pepuza was holy ground and the site to which Jerusalem should descend.

In their pre-millenarian views, however, they agreed with the general trend of the Christian thought of the period. The persecutions under Marcus Aurelius led to eschatological extravagances in all parts of the Church. The accusations of heterodoxy can in no case be proved. We may even say that the emphasis laid on the Paraclete added new meaning to a neglected Christian dogma, and was necessarily an influence against Monarchianism.

The later story of the ' heresy ' need not delay us. It had its martyrs, in spite of the statements of the Fathers to the contrary; and the bitterness of the orthodox is shown by the fact that in imprisonment for a common Christ they refused to hold any intercourse with the Montanist confessors. Communions of 'Tertullianists' are said to have been in existence in North Africa in the days of Augustine, and Montanism lingered on in Asia to the fourth century and later. The decision of the Synod of Constantinople (A.D. 381) with regard to them is pathetic reading : 'The Montanists or Phrygians we receive as we do pagans, namely, the first day we make them Christians, the second cate-chumens, the third day we exorcise them by breathing thrice into their face and ears and make them continue a good while in the church and hear the Scriptures, and afterwards we baptize them.'   So the devil was finally driven out from the 'heretics.'

> 'At last in the sixth century the Emperor Justinian resolved to stamp them out, and the historian Pro-copius tells us that in their despair the Montanists gathered themselves, with their wives and children, into their churches, and, setting fire to the buildings, perished in the flames rather than submit to the bishops' Church, which had urged the persecution through all these centuries, and had forbidden the members to have any communion with the Montanists, even when confined in a common prison for a common faith.' [1]

By such means is the City of God set up on earth.

In conclusion we may put for our own encouragement the opinions of Wesley and Renan on this subject side by side.   Here we have the view of the typical man of the world :

> 'An unrestrained credulity, a limitless belief in the

[1] Lindsay, *Church and the Ministry*, p. 244.

gifts of the Spirit, made Montanism one of the most extreme types of fanaticism known in all the history of man.'

Welsey in his day heard much on the subject of fanaticism and enthusiasm: the clergy of the Church of England seemed to spend most of their time in his day, so far as we can gather, in denouncing these evils. It is interesting therefore to read in the pages of the *Journal* under the date Wednesday, August 15, 1750:

> 'By reflecting on an odd book which I had read on this journey, *The General Delusion of Christians with regard to Prophecy*, I was fully convinced of what I had long suspected, 1. That the Montanists, in the second and third centuries, were real, scriptural Christians; and 2. That the grand reason why the miraculous gifts were so soon withdrawn, was not only that faith and holiness were well nigh lost; but that dry, formal, orthodox men began even then to ridicule whatever gifts they had not themselves; and to decry them all, as either madness or imposture.'

Space forbids our following out the parallel with the Methodist movement as another phenomenon of irregular prophesying, also with many similar movements in the Middle Ages. The influence of Montanism on the Church in increased ascetic severity and fear of prophetic extravagances must also be admitted.

III

THE CULT OF ST. FRANCIS

FIFTY years ago, Ernest Renan said with characteristic cheerfulness : ' I am the only man of my time that has been able to comprehend Jesus and Francis of Assisi.' Since these words were spoken the records of the lives of both the Great Master and His disciple have been submitted to the most rigorous criticism. After this long process of education, it is at least conceivable that we are able to understand St. Francis, and even his Great Model, almost as well as M. Renan himself. It is at any rate certain that Francis, most winsome and most human of saints, has become a popular hero. Protestants have vied with Catholics in their enthusiastic praise of the Little Poor Man of Assisi. When the Salvation Army issues a popular life of a Roman Catholic saint, we may well inquire the reason for so strange a phenomenon.

The *Imitation of Christ* has long been a favourite devotional handbook among all varieties of Christians. Yet those quiet musings of cloistered virtue, shielded from the rough blasts of the world, could hardly stir men's spirits as the living Word itself. The Middle Age produced its real ' Imitation ' not in the walks of some German monastery, but under the blue sky of Italy, on the hills of Umbria, in the sunshine and among the flowers. The real ' Imitation ' must be lived among the haunts of sin and sorrow, as it was in the villages of Galilee or in the narrow streets of Jerusalem.

To this day the motto of the Franciscan Order is taken from the great words of Paul, 'God forbid that I should glory save in the cross of our Lord Jesus Christ.' The Brothers Minor have wandered far from that ideal in many stages of their history, but it was the actual interpretation of the life of Francis. Bonaventura, one of his early biographers, was right in spirit, if not in detail, when he described seven occasions on which the Cross was specially connected with the life of Francis as the seal of God in him. ' Lo,' he says, ' by these seven appearances of the Cross of Christ in thee and about thee thou hast attained, as though by six steps, unto that seventh wherein thou dost make an end and rest.' One can hardly think that the stern asceticism and rigorous self-immolation which characterized the life of Francis is the element in it which our modern age finds so alluring. What is it then in him and in the early Franciscans which appeals so strongly to the twentieth century ?

We must begin by pointing out that in Francis himself we have a personality of exquisite simplicity and charm. So penetrating was its influence that the most impressionable of his early disciples bear evident traces of it in their own lives. The Franciscan spirit has become a definite and easily recognizable temper. What a difference is there in this respect between the two great contemporary orders of preaching Friars—the Franciscans and the Dominicans ! The Dominican Order displays in all its constitution and character the hall-mark of the Church—Dominic himself never manifests his presence there; but the Franciscan Order, in its original form, is Francis walking and talking in our midst. During his lifetime he was the darling of the people because of the very sweetness of his character; and after his death we turn to the records of his life under the spell of the same attractiveness.

The evils of his age which seem to us most noteworthy
are those of ecclesiasticism and superstition; an ecclesiasticism which seemed on the verge of committing suicide
by its very extravagance; and a superstition which seemed
dangerously near lunacy by its very absurdity. Ecclesiasticism made its most exalted claims in the great Pope,
Innocent III, who shut the gates of eternal life against the
populations of England and of France by the mere issue of
his papal interdicts. But the abuses of the corrupt ecclesiastical system were even more deplorable than the
arrogant claims of a strong doctrinaire like Innocent.
The monastic orders were turning away from their first
ideals, and the rigid rule of celibacy was bringing in a sad
reaction of loose living and worldliness. The Church
appealed to the awe, but scarcely to the intelligence, of
men. Her worship was but a constant repetition of a
glorified piece of legerdemain,—to

> . . . hear the blessed mutter of the mass
> And see God made and eaten all day long,
> And feel the steady candle-flame, and taste
> Good strong, thick stupefying incense-smoke !

If the saving elements of sincerity and pure living had been
present, even with such a worship the Church would have
been powerful for good. But neither purity nor sincerity
was a marked characteristic of the clergy. When some of
the great monasteries attracted customers to their festivals
by jugglers and harlots, it seems clear that the love of
money rather than the purity of the ascetic ideal was the
dominant motive. The records of the lives of the saints
are crowded with instances of what we should term the
most grotesque inventions. But such was the credulity or
superstition of the age that such fables were readily believed.
In the diocese of Liège the devoted Christina Mirabilis was

so carried away by ecstatic meditation that she was continually flying to the tops of lonely towers and trees to roost with the birds. ' At times, under the divine inspiration, she would roll up like a hedgehog; and when her relatives wished to secure her, they employed a man to hunt her like a bird. After a long chase across country, he succeeded in bringing her down with a blow of his bludgeon that broke her shin. When a few miracles had been wrought to vindicate her aerostatic mission, she was allowed to fly about in peace. She has occupied ever since the first place in the ornithology of Roman Catholic saintship.' That also was the golden age of relic worship. The arms and the legs, the toes and the fingers, the hair and the nails of defunct saints daily worked the most extraordinary miracles. Can it be wondered that this Age of Faith was also, if one examines it more carefully, an age of scepticism ? The more spiritual souls turned from the absurdities and puerilities and greed of the Church to the refuge of mysticism. In the South of Italy, Joachim of Flora taught that the Age of the Spirit was about to dawn. The first age had been the age of nettles, the second of roses, but this age was to be the age of lilies. With his new millenarian hopes he awakened the expectation of many simple, pious spirits. Others turned to the heretical movements which longed for Church reform and a simpler life—the Poor Men of Lyons and the Waldenses. The more radical thinkers who attacked the dogma of the Church linked themselves with the sect of the Cathari.

The Franciscan movement had some points of contact with the first two Societies, but by its dislike for theological speculation was entirely opposed to the last-named heresy. It was one of the weaknesses of Francis that he was opposed to secular and religious learning; yet, curiously enough, two of his immediate followers at least, Antony of Padua and Bonaventura, were great doctors of the Church; and none of the religious orders in later times produced greater scholars than the Franciscan Order. Francis himself was wont to say : ' My brethren who are led by desire of learning shall find their hands empty in the time of tribulation. For them books shall be useful for nothing, and shall be thrown in windows and cupboards.' The strict rule of the order forbade any kind of property to the friars—not even books, the last solace of the forlorn, could they possess. A certain novice, who longed to have a Psalter for himself, once went to beg leave from Francis. But the saint spoke of the Emperor Charles the Great and his renowned heroes, Roland and Oliver, and the Paladins, who fought against the Moors ' with much travail and sweat to the death.' Far better were it to copy their example than to record or read their deeds. A few days later the novice came again and renewed his request as Francis was sitting by the fire, and this time Francis replied : ' After you have a Psalter you will desire and wish to have a Breviary. Then you will sit in your chair like a great prelate and say to your brother : " Bring me the Breviary." ' Then stooping down he picked up a handful of ashes and scattered them on the head of the novice, saying : ' Go, that is your Breviary, that is your Psalter.'

Over against the Church's avarice and love of money Francis set the ideal of absolute *poverty*—a literal representation of the apostolic life. His call to service came to him on February 24, 1209, as the priest read the words of Jesus in the celebration of the mass at the Portiuncula of Assisi. Church and priest faded far away into the dim background. Jesus, his crucified Lord, was speaking directly to him : ' Wherever ye go, preach, saying, " The kingdom of heaven is at hand. Heal the sick, cleanse the lepers, cast out devils. Freely ye have received, freely give. Provide neither silver nor gold nor brass in your purses, neither scrip nor two coats, nor shoes nor staff : for the labourer is worthy of his meat." ' From that moment Francis lived a life of literal obedience to the words of Jesus. A hut of rude planks he would reject as his shelter, because it was too grand for the servant of the Carpenter; so he would build himself a shelter of branches of trees, again to be forsaken when one of his friars inadvertently termed it ' thy cell.' This was in honour of that Son of man who ' had not where to lay His head.' His biographers have probably wrested the story of his life to make it a perfect reproduction of the Gospel narratives. We must consider the story of his twelve followers and of the stigmata with that fact in mind. Leo tells us how on his death-bed he broke bread and distributed it to the friars, as the perfect imitator of his Lord. The physician who attended him at the last was Good John of Arezzo. Francis addressed him as ' Bembenignate ' in his quaint fashion, never calling him by his name, out of reverence to Him who said, ' There is none good but one.' So he would never call any one ' Father ' or ' Master,' out of reverence to the Lord who said, ' Call no man father upon earth, and be not ye called masters.' Sometimes this literal spirit became amusing, as when Francis forbade the brother who did the cooking to put dried beans into water at night for the next day's dinner, because of the words, ' Take no thought for the morrow.' Nevertheless we can easily see how this spectacle of absolute renunciation of wealth on the part of hundreds and thousands of men, many of whom had been rich and of noble birth, stirred the imagination and awoke the conscience of Europe as nothing else could have done in such a money-loving age.

We must not be misled by the biographies in ascertaining what the reply of Francis was to the *ecclesiasticism* of the age. True, he was the devoted son of the Church, and most shrewd in spite of his simplicity. He knew that his work could only be done in alliance with the ecclesiastical authority. Therefore he sought the approval of the Pope and the protection of the great Cardinal Ugolini. Always he taught the friars to be humble towards the clergy, to reverence every Church. 'Learn, brethren, that the gain of souls is most pleasing to God, and this we can better obtain when in peace, than in discord with the clergy.' When friars came to him complaining that certain bishops would not permit them to preach, and begging him to obtain a special licence from the Pope, he replied : ' I wish by perfect humility and reverence first to convert the prelates.' He showed them the advantages of example over precept as a means of converting others. He sent out friars with ' fair and clean pyxes to honourably preserve the Body of the Lord,' and in all ways reverenced the teachings of the Church. Yet we may well doubt whether the picture of perfect obedience which is found in a corpse, without will and without resistance, really originated with Francis. His own obedience was never of that rigid and dehumanized character. However obedient and docile a servant of the Church he may have seemed, the whole spirit of his movement was in direct antagonism to the central principle of ecclesiasticism. He sent a company of laymen up and down Italy preaching the Gospel, exercising a privilege which then belonged only to the bishops. He, a layman, consecrated Clare to the religious life. He proclaimed that the essence of that life was in the imitation of Christ and not in any ritual or creed whatsoever. A beautiful story tells how one day a poor old woman, who had two sons in the order, came to beg an alms from the friars. But alas ! all their wealth was the New Testament from which they read the lessons at matins. ' Give the

Testament to our mother,' said Francis, ' that she may sell
it for her necessity; for I believe firmly that it will please
the Lord and the Blessed Virgin more than if we were to
read in it.'   Such a spirit as that is a danger to merely
churchly ideals; and it was undoubtedly by the plotting of
the ' evil prelates,' as Leo terms them, that Francis was
induced to resign his position as minister-general of the
order at the chapter held in September, 1220.

We must not allow the fact of the celibacy of the friars,
nor the later perversions of the biographers, to mislead us in
regard to their attitude towards women.   The idea that
Francis never gazed upon the face of woman, so held was he
by the monastic ideal, must be pure myth.   From one of
the earliest sources we learn that the first friars sometimes
shared the repast of the sisters, even eating from the same
porringer.   In the *Fioretti* we have a pretty story of the
feast at which Saint Francis and Saint Clare joined together
with one of the companions of Saint Francis and one companion of Saint Clare, and all the other companions took
each his place at the table with all humility.   By his order
of Tertiaries Francis consecrated and blessed the purity of
family life.   The first member of that order was said to
have been a certain wealthy corn-merchant, Lucchese of
Caggiano, who had made his money by an unscrupulous
corner in grain.   At his conversion he sold much of his
property and gave it to the poor, keeping a modest com-
petence for himself and his wife.   No poor man ever went
away from that house empty-handed, and his liberality was
known far and wide.   One day in despair his wife said:
' Where am I to find bread to give them, O brainless head,
weakened with fasting?'   ' In the bin, my Buonadonna,'
answered her husband, ' be as good in act as you are in
name; trust Him who fed the five thousand with five loaves
and two small fishes.'   His Buonadonna obeyed, and sure

enough on opening the bin it was full of loaves.   Sabatier
tells the story of the death of this couple in a most beautiful
fashion.   When in 1260 Lucchese saw her gradually fading
away, his grief was too great to be endured.

> ' " You know, dear companion," he said to her,
> when she had received the last sacraments, " how
> much we have loved one another while we could
> serve God together : why should we not remain
> united until we depart to the ineffable joy ? Wait
> for me. I also will receive the sacraments and go to
> heaven with you." So he spoke, and called back the
> priest to administer them to him.   Then after holding
> the hands of his dying companion, comforting her
> with gentle words, when he saw that her soul was
> gone he made over her the sign of the cross, stretched
> himself beside her, and calling with love upon Jesus,
> Mary, and St. Francis, he fell asleep for eternity.'

Who can say that the Franciscan ideal in its simplicity had
a false idea of woman, in the presence of such a picture as
that ?

Innocent III did his best to turn the friars into monks;
but he never succeeded. The dominant religious ideal of
the monastic life was so strong as to have considerably
influenced the Franciscans, but it never absorbed them.
Again and again Francis was led away from the haunts of
men in a hunger for solitude and religious contemplation.
'In preaching,' he said, ' the spiritual feet wax dusty, and
many things distract a man, and discipline is relaxed.'
Was he to renounce his evangelistic work altogether ?   He
appealed to the brethren, and then to Clare and Silvester,
an early disciple. Both of them replied that it was the
Lord's will that the herald of Christ should go forth to

preach.   From that mission the early friars never wavered. One of them had a vision of a countless host of men stricken with blindness, with their faces uplifted to heaven, on bended knees, lifting up their hands to God, with tears beseeching His mercy and light.   And there came a great radiance from heaven and illumined all—it was the Order of the Brothers Minor.   So they went out as evangelists, working with the peasants in the fields and talking of the love of God, mingling with the lepers and washing their sores, crying aloud as prophets in the streets of the cities of Italy and Europe.   The closest parallel to their activities is found in the early Methodist preachers, and the spiritual results of both these great revivals may fittingly be compared.   The Methodists sang :

> We have no abiding city here,
> But see a city out of sight.

Lucido, the brother minor, was unwilling to stay in one place for a month; but when it pleased him to stay in any place, immediately he went away, saying, ' We have no dwelling-place here, but in heaven.'   The round preacher did not beg for alms in the fashion of the Brothers Minor, but fed at the homes of the people to whom he ministered in his itinerary, and was rewarded with £12 per annum in addition.   He, too, was wedded to his Lady Poverty.

Let us not allow the asceticism of the movement to obscure the evangelism and charity which were of its essence.   Even the austerities of the life at Rivo-Torto or the Portiuncula were modified by common sense.   One midnight, at the former home, the friars were disturbed by one of their number crying aloud that he was dying of hunger.   In their new enthusiasm they were wont to afflict their bodies beyond measure. None of them exceeded Francis in rigour towards ' his brother the ass,'

D

as he termed his body.   Yet he bade them all rise and join
in a meal with the one who disturbed them, lest he should
be ashamed to eat alone.   On another occasion he cured a
sick friar by joining him in eating grapes, encouraging him
against any fear of self-indulgence by his own example.
The abuses of the so-called religious life of that age could
not have been cured in any more effective way than by such
a life as that of Francis.   His transparent goodness, his
absolute self-denial, his simple directness, his spiritual
fervour, his saving gift of common sense, made him the
very incarnation of all that was best in Christianity as
applied to the Church of the thirteenth century.

We must remember, however, that the period in which
Francis lived and died was not merely an age of ecclesiasticism and superstition, it was the great age of *chivalry*.
Romantic dreams and achievements were the common meat
and drink.   The air was full of songs of love and adventure.
The gay minstrel moved from court to castle and from
castle to camp.   The knight-errant rode abroad in quest
of high renown.   An age of dreamers and idealists; when
the vision of the Holy Sepulchre could set men's hearts
ablaze to win Jerusalem, when even the children set out on
their crusade of sorrow.   Men revived the stories of the
Knights of the Table Round, and the Paladins of Charle-
magne loomed large as Hercules in earlier myths.   Francis
was the son of a merchant—one of that class who were the
bankers and the news-carriers of the world.   If any man
were full of romantic stories, that man would be the wealthy
merchant who moved from castle to castle and was almost
received as an equal by the nobility.   Francis may have
received his very name from his father's love for France.
At any rate, the gay spirit of French romanticism entered
into his very blood.   He was for ever singing the songs of
France, and turning the art of the minstrel to God's uses.

'Sometimes he picked up a branch from the earth, and, laying it on his left arm, he drew in his right hand another stick like a bow over it as if on a viol or other instrument, and, making fitting gestures, sang with it in French unto the Lord Jesus Christ.' On the morning of his great renunciation, when he had left home, parents, wealth, clothes, and all behind, he turned his back on Assisi, and fared away through the woods to a friendly monastery. On his way he chanted praises to the Lord in the French tongue, when he was assailed by robbers, who asked him who he was. 'I am the herald of the great King,' said Francis. But they threw the herald of God into a ditch of snow and left him more forlorn than ever. Yet the true Franciscan sang his praises in the direst trials and the sorest straits of hunger and destitution. When Francis on his death-bed was deprived of instruments of music, God took pity on him, we are told, and sent His angels to give him so wondrous a concert as was never heard on earth before. Dying he continued to sing far on into the night, and when he was wearied out he begged his comrades Angelo and Leo to go on. He went to meet God singing. He overcame the bitter sorrows of his life by that note of gay gladness which was so characteristic of his truest followers. They were the real minstrels, the real troubadours of the Lord. Pacifico, the King of Verses, was especially 'a truly courteous teacher of singers.' The happy note of simple gladness and of quaint humour which we constantly find among the Minorites was derived from Francis himself. He loved to call that great-hearted giant Leo, 'God's little lamb.' Such was his love for his early followers that he spared them the labour of collecting alms until they begged to join his toil. So they went out one by one through villages and towns. Back they came in merry and jocund fashion, saying one to another, 'I have more alms than thou.' And Francis rejoiced with their simple jollity. His own romantic spirit fired their enthusiasm. No Crusader went on a more perilous expedition than did Francis and Illuminato, who moved from the camp of the Christians to the camp of the Saracens, in the vain attempt to win the Soldan as a convert for Christ. The love of adventure was satisfied by these religious spirits, who could not be cooped up in monasteries, but wandered into the remote corners of Europe as the knights of Christ. Angelo was the first knight to come into the order; but all in a knightly spirit, for the great love of their Lady Poverty, wandered abroad, redressing human wrong. In the *Fioretti* we have a story of a tender youth who was tempted to return to the world soon after he joined the Order. To him God gave a wondrous vision of 'a countless multitude of saints, like a procession, two and two, clad in beautous robes of precious stuffs.' Two of them were marked out by special garments, and near the end of the procession was one adorned with great glory that seemed a new-made knight. He was much afraid, but, summoning up his courage, he ran after the last of them to ask who they were and learned they were the Brothers Minor, coming from the glory of Paradise; and the two distinguished ones were St. Francis and St. Antony; and the last one was an honoured brother who had lately died, a faithful knight of Christ, led in triumph to the glory of Paradise, because he had so valiantly fought against temptations. Francis said that the humble and faithful friars were his brethren of the Table Round who lay hidden in deserts and obscure places. *Courtesy* and *chivalry* were marks of the true knight, and Francis exemplified both every day of his life. He was the champion of the poor and the oppressed, and in all his actions the perfect gentleman. 'Courtesy is one of the qualities of God Himself,' he said, 'who of His courtesy giveth His sun and His rain to the just and the unjust.' Before his conversion, when setting out in high spirits on an expedition to the South of Italy, he met a soldier of noble birth, but poor and ill-clad; with his usual impulsiveness Francis surrendered his own rich apparel to the poor knight. The law forbade lepers to appear on public highways, and the friars tended them in the lazarettos. But one good simpleton led a sorely ulcerated leper out to the Portiuncula, and, meeting Francis, was gently reproved : ' You ought not to lead out these Christians, because it is neither decent for you nor for them.' Immediately his tender heart was grieved; he had caused pain to the leper. Back he goes with him to the leper-house, and for penance, to show his spirit of brotherhood, he eats out of one bowl with the loathsome and repellent sufferer. The heart of all courtesy is there. Can we wonder that a man who could so interpret the most popular ideals of his age, and apply them so practically to the religious life, should be the object of his country's adoration ?

In his *love of nature*, as well as in his love of music, he was the true child of the South. All the creatures of God were his brothers and sisters; lambs and doves and larks were his special favourites. If he had a chance of an interview with the Emperor, he would say, he knew what the subject of conversation should be. He would ask for an edict forbidding any one to kill or snare his sisters the larks, and exhorting all, even on Christmas Day, to make special provision for them and the oxen and asses. Flowers also filled his soul with rapture, and he begged the gardener to leave room there for green herbs which in their time should produce flowers for the friars, for the love of Him who is called ' the flower of the field ' and ' the lily of the valley.' Surely Francis is the true Romantic, and, because of his adventurous chivalry, his boundless sympathy with God's creation in humanity and nature, he provided the best

possible outlet for the energies of his age as well as the
most complete answer to the defects of the Church.

The picture of corruption in the Church and of chivalry
in the State is by no means a true representation of the
twelfth and thirteenth centuries.   Church and State were
not so clearly divided from each other.   Dignitaries of the
Church were great feudal lords, and all men were regarded
as sons and daughters of one Holy Mother, the Church.
We should correct our idea of the nobility, as knights of
chivalry, by a closer examination of the *feudal system*.   Its
harsh pressure upon the serfs, which kept them at the beck
and call of some liege lord to be hurried into some personal
feud at a moment's notice, was intolerable.   One petty
lord was for ever fighting with another petty lord, and in
so doing only copying the bad example of his superiors.
The state of war between certain cities of Italy was a chronic
one.   The greatest sufferers from the wars of the nobility,
and the exactions both of the feudal lords and the Papacy,
were the common people.   With the Crusades had come the
development of commerce with the East and the birth of
the middle-classes.   This was the signal for the decay
of the feudal system.   With the growth of a trading
community in the towns of Western Europe, there grew
up the added feud of rich and poor.   This was specially
prominent in the cities of Italy.   They were divided almost
universally into the two camps of Majores and Minores, rich
and poor.   It is significant that Francis threw himself
enthusiastically into the ranks of the poor, and called his
followers ' Fratres Minores,' the Brothers Minor.   In their
preaching they became continually the mouthpiece of the
oppressed.   In Francis the poor found a leader, a champion,
almost an avenger.   Thoughts which they scarcely dared
to whisper, he proclaimed in the market-place.   The services
of the Church were, of course, in Latin, which was even

then largely unintelligible to the Italians. Francis and his followers spoke and preached in the language of the people, and for their dress they adopted with but little change the coarse greyish-brown robe of the peasants of Umbria. Rich and poor were bound together in the ranks of the Friars in one brotherhood without respect of persons. Noble and peasant were alike in that fraternity. The story of the *Fioretti*, which tells how Saint Louis, the holy King of France, went on a pilgrimage to Perugia that he might hold fellowship with the humble friar Giles may not be true, but it is significant of much that even its narration should be possible. An age which could dream of king and beggar in familiar embrace, because of their common love of God, had indeed ' seen distant gates of Eden gleam.'

With the Crusades also came in the sad plague of leprosy, for which science had no cure, and for which legislation had no hope. The only method of dealing with these unhappy sufferers, which the ' Dark Ages ' could suggest, was to read the burial service over them and drive them out from the homes and haunts of men to cling to the skirts of society, an abhorrence and a terror. The very first work of Francis and his friars was to turn to these neglected sufferers, to mingle with them as brethren, caring both for their spiritual and temporal needs. By the new spirit which the Franciscans introduced in their dealings with the outcast leper, the horrors of this great scourge were gradually reduced throughout the West. In thinking of the friars as social and political reformers, however, we must put in the place of first importance the creation of the Third Order. This was done to bring the religious life out of the monastery and away from the officials of the Church, who were supposed to be the sole representatives of it, to the life of the family and the home. Its vows were of a very simple character.

'It required the banishment of hatred, the cultivation of a loving spirit, the restitution of ill-gotten gain, the profession of the Catholic Faith, and earnest effort to obey God's commandments; it inculcated the duty of confession and communion three times a year, the wearing of plain garments and avoidance of worldly assemblies, the keeping of the fast, if possible, in Advent and Lent, and, when possible, the recitation of the Divine Office.'

By this order Francis became the true pastor of the people, who could, alas, say with only too much truth, 'No man careth for my soul.' But with practical sagacity Francis inserted three clauses in the rule, which struck the death-blow at the feudal system in Italy. The Tertiaries were forbidden to carry arms, except in defence of Church or native country. How then could they respond to the call of their feudal lord whose whim it was to chastise his neighbour? They were also forbidden to take oaths, even the oath of fealty to their feudal superior. The result of these stringent regulations, enthusiastically welcomed by the people and supported by the enormous influence of the Papacy, was that within three years of the death of Francis the power of feudalism was broken in Italy.[1] The rule also insisted that collections should be made among the members of the Third Order for the relief of the poorer brethren. This was the foundation of the system of what we term 'Trade Unions,' for it was a great union of the people against the oppression of the feudal lords. There is little wonder, therefore, that Francis takes his place as the Patron Saint of all Social Reforms, and to-day many of the Unions of Italy display his name on their banners. What a contrast

[1] Cf. Knox Little *in loc*. It is fair to say, however, that the point of view here represented is by no means universally accepted.

is presented between the Italy of Francis, which responded so warmly to his gospel for the poor, and the modern Italy with its strong antagonism to the ideals of the Church. M. Paul Sabatier, in his Jowett Lecture on Modernism, gave a moving account of an incident of which he was a spectator :

'On July 7, 1907, the day of the Garibaldi commemoration, I was in Florence,' he says. 'The people's enthusiasm was at its height. The Archbishop's palace, the glittering Cathedral of Santa Maria del Fiore, and the Baptistery, those houses of God, built of old by the people and for the people, remained silent, jealously closed and bereft of decoration. The people wished to mark their sense of this abstention and antithesis. Towards evening they marched through the cities in hundreds of companies. They decided that on passing the cathedral and Archbishop's palace they would return silence for silence, disdain for disdain. On reaching the piazza, the singing and the music ceased : in front of the palace flags and banners were silently lowered, the points towards the ground in token of reprobation. I shall never forget the spectacle, the Church no longer understanding the people whom she had brought up, and the people wounded by their mother and their teacher in their deepest instincts, in their patriotic religion. The march past was almost at an end, when all at once, up at the top of the blind and mute archiepiscopal residence, a little window suddenly opened. A head appeared, a hand waved a flag—the tri-coloured flag of free and united Italy—and in the great silence, which was increased by the people's astonishment, a cry fell, " Evviva l'Italia ! "—" Long live Italy ! "

In the twinkling of an eye the Garibaldian procession had halted, flags and banners were raised again. A tremendous cheer rang out, and in the eyes of many of these men who a moment before had been angry and bitter, there glistened tears of joy.'

If, once again, the Church could discover the secret which Francis learned, of winning completely the love and confidence of the people, she would again go forth on her miraculous mission to heal the sick, cleanse the lepers, cast out devils. What the meditative writer of the *Imitatio* said in his day is just as true to-day: 'Christ Jesus hath had many lovers of His heavenly kingdom, but few bearers of His cross.' This is an age which manufactures few saints, but is lavish in its adornment of their tombs. Francis would exhort us to *be* a Roland or an Oliver rather than to record their career. Nevertheless, an age which can be so enthusiastic in its regard for so pure a love as that of Francis cannot be entirely destitute of those elements which blended to make him what he was.

IV

THE LOLLARDS IN THE TIME
OF RICHARD II

> The lanterne of lyghtte
> Non fulget luce serena;
> Yt ys not alle aryght
> Populus bibit ecce venena.

So sang a poet ' On the Times ' of Richard II, and although
there have always been men to say ' the times are out of
joint,' then certainly it was a fact that ' Yt ys not alle aryght.'
The laconic entrances in the official Patent Rolls are eloquent
of the reigning state of disorder—wars and rumours of
wars, murder, rapine, and assault with very tardy justice.
The King's peace was not kept, and the quarrels and intrigues
at Court strangled the central authority, whilst in the
country bands of retainers defied all justice in maintaining
the brigandage of their lords. England had been convulsed
by a social revolution which led to the death of the Archbishop and the Chancellor of England, but the Parliament
which should have dealt with the Peasants' Rising of 1381,
devoted its attention primarily to the settlement of a private
feud between the Duke of Lancaster and the Earl of North-
umberland. The country groaned under the heavy taxation
of a useless war, whilst the French without hindrance
continued to ravage the south coasts of England. Life
was not the secure and commonplace thing it is to-day.
The roads were thronged by wayfarers of all sorts and conditions, peasants out of bond, Friars, pilgrims, merchants,

whilst the woods gave shelter to a strange company of cut-purse and hermit. This throng moved down the road of life in a half darkness, for the time of stress and strain in State and Society was also a time of religious depression— 'the lanterne of lyghtte' had flickered and grown dim. The Church no longer gave light to guide the steps of earth's pilgrims. She was in serious danger of forfeiting her spiritual significance, and God's tribute was never more prone to find its way into Cæsar's coffers. Religious life had lost the sense of reality, and, as always with such a calamity, the spirit had fled and left rule and letter sovereign. Bishops were wonderfully orthodox, but were often great magnates of the world and leaders of very earthly armies. The Bishop of Norwich gloried in his 'crowds of slain' at Gravelines and Dunkirk when on crusade against the schismatic Pope Clement VII. The monastic chronicler, Walsingham, is loud in his praise of these crusaders and 'the victory of the Cross': 'They marched forward towards the town sparing no one but striving to destroy them to the last man—and such was the potency of the Cross that the crusaders most gloriously took possession of the town and so destroyed the enemies of the Cross that not one amongst them escaped with his life.' The universal Church was torn by schism, and was busy settling its differences by means of the temporal arm. The greatest sin of the 'enemies of the Cross of Christ' was that they called the Head of the Church Clement instead of Urban, and had had the misfortune to become involved in the quarrel between England and France. These warrior bishops went gorgeously apparelled and kept up great retinues on the tithes of an oppressed people. The Church was losing her sympathy with the people. Here is a contemporary picture of the English labourer: 'Poor men who may not pay rents to lords and their dymes and offerings to curates, and maintain their wife and child and live out of debt travail they never so busily night and day.' ' Lady Mede' had her devotees in all ranks of the clergy, and the religious orders were idle and mercenary. The Friars had forgotten the ideals of St. Francis and were suffering from the evils of mendicancy, whilst profession of poverty went side by side with growing luxury. The songs of the period are loud in their hatred and ridicule of the Friars, and the people were ready to stone their quondam friends. The priest had discovered that sin might be a lucrative evil, in fact, a blessing in disguise, and the poet would find many appreciative listeners among the Friars' victims :

> Thai say thet thai distroye synne
> And thai mayntene men moste therinne.

And again :

> A cure of soule they care not fore,
> So that they mowe much money take.

The times cried out for some physician to restore a healthy tone and spirit and the Lollard movement came into being as a protest against such mockery and negligence. The Lollard priest stood for reality in religion, and his programme was ' to bere his shepe til his backe bend.' The movement was the first step which England took towards dissent, and it bears all the marks of a new venture. The Lollards of Richard II's day were not quite prepared to die for the hope that was in them, but rather met persecution with recantation and with a speedy disappearance to some other part of England. There was no rigid organization in the new sect, but its followers had a certain resemblance in cast of mind and in creed. The main characteristic of the Lollard was that of ' the preacher ' simply, and it was only at Salisbury that any Church organization was attempted. Preachers may be scholars or peasants, and the

Lollardy of Oxford birth was cherished by ploughman and artisan in the country. The University was purged of its heresy, and the leading academic Lollards were not long in forsaking the new way, but ' the sawynge of mennes soulis ' was a message of true democracy, and was not without lasting appeal to the lower orders.

Leicester, Hereford, and London were the three chief centres of this expelled Lollardy. Northampton shows itself almost a Lollard town, Salisbury attempts the ordination of its ministers, whilst Nottingham, York, Bristol, Coventry, Reading, and Chichester have also Lollard communities. Wales yields an asylum for the hunted from Herefordshire, and there is an interesting mention of Ireland in the Patent Rolls of 1388–1392. It was natural that Leicestershire should become a centre for the spread of Wyclif's doctrines, for it was to Lutterworth that he retired after his expulsion from Oxford, and in this country his teaching struck such root that the death of the master in 1384 did not mean the death of Lollardy—' there shall never be one lost good.'

The Leicester canon, in the *Knighton Chronicle*, complains bitterly of Lollard activity—there was ' never so much discord as now in these parts.' He has heard and seen the preachers, and his chronicle shows the swing of the movement—there is unbounded energy, desire to preach the new sect by every way and means, and a general ' throwing off of ease from the body.' There is never a good word for a Friar, and the preaching is always of the doctrines of Wyclif. The monastic chronicler is in despair : ' These opinions were appropriated by all and spread far and wide '; ' you scarcely could meet two men in the road but one of them was a disciple of Wyclif.' Outside Leicester there stood an old chapel dedicated to St. John the Baptist. It became a place of retreat and communion, where the new tenets were discussed and the curious were ever welcome. Richard Waytestathe and William Smith, the chief inhabitants, showed no reverence for the sacred house where they were lodged. When in need of firewood to cook some vegetables they burned the image of St. Katherine which still adorned the chapel, and made merry over the sacrilege—it is to be a second martyrdom for Katherine, and perhaps will give her a chance of heaven. Lollardy was getting hold of the people, and herein lay its strength. The monastic chronicler, with his love for authority and decorum, writes down William Smith as of weak intellect; his love troubles have turned his head. But it is possible to read in him the serious man who finds life's pleasures fail him, but discovers what he seeks in the Lollard doctrines and sets himself to learn to read and write and takes a new interest in life : ' In those days the sect was held in great honour outside the wall.' In 1389 the Lollard community at Leicester was so aggressive that the Archbishop of Canterbury visited the diocese and excommunicated the heretics. The names of the accused give the status of the Lollard community there. The Church could make short work of such enemies as William Smith, Richard Waytestathe (chaplain), Robert Dexter and his wife, Nicolas Tailor, M. Scryvener, John Harry, William Parchmener, and Roger Goldsmith. They held Lollard opinions as to tithes, images, a priest in mortal sin, confession and the Friars, and had sought to spread their views in the surrounding country, but the authority of King and Archbishop was too strong, and the humble fraternity was discredited. From these simple folk William Swynderby, who was to become an important man in Herefordshire, learned his first Lollardy. He was transformed from the hermit of the woods, with a grievance against the world, into the silver-tongued preacher of the countryside : ' The people

cherished him like another God.' This prophet of the new
faith was too popular to be left at large, and although
persecution at first gained him new adherents when he
preached on the high-road from an impromptu pulpit of
stones ' in the teeth of the bishop,' yet he is finally checked
with excommunication and threat of death by fire. Swynderby retreats to Coventry, and we next hear of him in the
west of England. Melton, Loughborough, and Harborough
had heard his voice, now Monmouth and Hereford gave the
discredited prophet a warm welcome. He is in Monmouth
in 1390, and there receives letters from the Bishop of Hereford warning him not to preach. In August of the same
year he preaches a notable sermon at Whitney (Herefordshire), of which the lord of the town keeps a copy in his
enthusiasm. Many times Swynderby is cited to appear
before the Bishop of Hereford, but the official entry shows
that he evaded the honour : ' William Swynderby is long
looked for.' The King and the Archbishop of Canterbury
supplement the efforts of the Bishop of Hereford, but the
Patent Rolls for 1392 show Swynderby's success in defying
authority : ' To John Bishop of Hereford on his petition
informing the King that although empowered by letters
patent authorizing the Archbishop of Canterbury to arrest
all preachers of unsound doctrine he has convicted William
Swynderby and Stephen Belle to be excommunicated
preaching in diverse parts of his diocese, yet he has been
unable to do justice upon them either by ecclesiastical
censures or by force of the King's commission, for they
have betaken themselves to the parts of Wales where
the commission does not run—with their abettors and
accomplices.'

This mandate points to a growing Lollard community
in Herefordshire. The authorities complain of ' tares
which have too long a time sprung up here in our diocese.'

One of William Swynderby's assured companions was a certain Walter Brute, whose name finds its way into one of the popular songs of the day, ' The Creed of Piers Ploughman.' He himself is described as ' lay-man and learned,' and his answers in Latin are of voluminous bulk, with many references to Scripture and to the Fathers. Brute is summoned for trial but follows Swynderby's example of evasion, and calls forth mandates to the Mayor of Hereford, one Thomas Oldcastle, to bring the defaulter to justice. Brute is finally brought to book, recants his heresy, and makes public confession at the market-cross in Hereford. The witnesses at his trial bear witness to the extent of Lollard influence in the west country—they come from Llanwin (Montgomery), from English Byknore (Forest of Dean), and from Whiteborne (north of the Malvern Hills). Walter Brute was accused of ' lurking and running into corners ' when wanted for his heretical preaching by the authorities, and the deep woods and quiet glades of the Forest of Dean country would provide welcome shelter to the hunted Lollard. The spread of Lollardy in these west-country districts is especially important in the light of its later history, for it was in such atmosphere that the youth of Sir John Oldcastle was passed. He was Lord of the Manor of Almeley in Herefordshire, where William Swynderby had once been a vigorous preacher. The countryside was permeated with Lollard influence, and the towns were familiar with the travelling preachers. The future hero of the Lollard cause would receive many a vivid impression from trials in the Cathedral, a mayor under injunctions from the King, and open recantations in the market-place.

The streets of fourteenth-century London have their story of early Lollardy as well as the lanes of Leicestershire and the woods of Hereford. In the city it was to the lower orders that Lollardy appealed, and the chroniclers

E

lay stress on the zeal of ' the humble citizens ' or ' the most vile of the citizens.' Politics and religion were in close contact in London, and the people were alive and interested, even the Bishop of Rochester gives them credit for intelligence : ' in London there is greater devotion and the people are more intelligent—greater fruit may be expected from preaching.' The Lollard movement in London became connected with a political and municipal quarrel, the democratic party espousing the new dissent. The quarrel was one for free rights in the city between the lesser and the greater guilds. The victualling guilds, such as the fishmongers and the grocers, comprised the greater guilds, and had a monopoly of power in the city; invariably the mayor was chosen from amongst them, and they regulated the trade of the city to advantage their own pockets. John of Northampton led the lesser guilds of tailoring, drapers, &c., in a crusade against this monopoly of interest and power, and found that the tenets of the Lollards fitted well with his more democratic mind and aims for reform. The Chroniclers state that ' they were stirred up in this by John Wyclif and his followers in despite to the clergy.' For, strangely enough, the Church seemed the enemy of the people by its more aristocratic leanings in a people's quarrel. This connexion between the people's guilds and the London Lollards is borne out by other records of the times. King Richard's mandate to the mayor and sheriff of London in 1391, against those who cherish heretical opinions, describes the offenders as ' lay men and artisans.' It was a member of the lesser guilds who first introduced Lollardy at Northampton, ' James Collyn—sometime a prentice at the trade of Mersery in London refuseinge his arte to become a Lollard.' A Lollard tract denouncing monks and Friars shows the same bias, ' also it seemeth that merchant grocers and victuallers run in the same curse fully.'

In 1387 there is record of a typical Lollard disturbance in London, where doctrines of grace, sins of Friars, and class prejudice are strangely mingled, and are supported in addition by those who love any disturbance. A certain chaplain, Peter Pateshille, released from his order of Augustinian Friars, came in contact with Lollardy, and began to publish the crimes of his former brethren. Such a sermon would not want hearers, for the Friars were not loved in London or elsewhere. There were nearly a hundred Lollards gathered to hear Pateshille at the Church of St. Christopher, and there he ' vomited out the crimes of the Friars to the horror of those hearing.' The Friars of the Augustine convent soon heard what was on foot, and twelve of their number came to the church and were greatly disturbed by what they heard. One of them, more zealous for his Order than the rest, contradicted the preacher and gave the ideal opportunity for a demonstration. The Lollards rise with a rush and throw the Friar out, for the gentle art of eviction was understood quite well even then. The other eleven brothers follow, to be torn and beaten and lashed with angry words outside : ' We despise homicides, we will burn these Sodomites,' and then a curious patriotic turn, ' we will hang the traitors of the King and of England.' By such means Lollardy made headway in London. Malvern's chronicle pays it this tribute of importance : ' In full Parliament a great rumour broke out concerning the Lollards and their preaching, by which foolish and simple were perverted and even the rich were greatly infected with the Lollard opinions.' Some few of the knights of the Queen-Mother's household had espoused the Lollard cause, but their Lollardy was short-lived. Their agitation in 1395 brought King Richard back from Ireland and he soon put an end to their new opinions—the Lollards of England were to remain emphatically the People.

The above narrative of Lollard activity in England during the reign of Richard II gives some picture of the movement. Disturbed sermons and unseemly demonstrations, extravagant language and irreverence, flying Swynderbys and recanting Smiths scarcely suggest 'the vision splendid.' Yet behind all there is something true, noble, and eternal. Authority regarded the enthusiasts as seeking 'the utter destruction of order and good rule.' The orthodox regarded them as tares sown by the enemy in the fair garden of the Church. The popular minstrel called them heretics, schismatics and madmen in one. But the answer of Swynderby is convincing : 'For God wot for hele I did it of mine own and of the people, and that was in my mind. But sire it seems to me that ye charge not so greatly the breaking of God's hests as ye done of your own. And sire if it be your will in default that the people wanted you to teach them, and their curates did not, by the desire of the people that weren hungrie and thirsty after God's word each one to bear up others charge as God's Law bids—I preached—not for disobedience to you, but sire in fulfilling of the obedience that God's Law bids me to.' Here is a man who dares to set the priest aside and feel the burden of souls upon his own heart and conscience. The echo of the Lollard doctrine passed into Bohemia, and later to a canon of the order of St. Augustine, who dared to withstand Pope and Emperor 'in fulfilling of the obedience that God's Law bids me to.' The Methodists of the eighteenth century woke the strain again, 'Single yet undismayed I am, I dare believe in Jesu's name '—when shall we again hear it, for the memory of England is short ?

The Lollards were knit by a kind of freemasonry; they were emphatically people of the Way. Thorpe, a member of the community, expressed it as ' to feel right homely with one another,' and many other instances might be cited. William Smith in his chapel outside Leicester Wall welcomed all to his abode if their heart were as his, 'for here was hospitality and entertainment for all who came.' At Northampton there is the same report : 'all ribauds infected with Lollardy that came into the said toune are all courteously received and mainetayned as if they were prophets before all others.' From Herefordshire comes the same testimony to the friendship of those of the Way, 'For I come oft into men's houses,' remarks Swynderby the outlawed. The travelling preacher bound the sect together in mutual knowledge and sympathy, and was responsible for much of the 'family' feeling. The Lollard had all the excitement of bearing down on the preacher after his sermon and of carrying him off to the home for conversation and refreshment, or as a disbeliever puts it, 'and after the said maior and Lollardes with great pride and jollite ledd the fals preacher to the house of the Maior.' Wyclif had given his followers a prescription and a reason for such social intercourse 'that men should eaten in good measure that their wits be more sharp and they more able to serve God.' It is not the ascetic who speaks, but the friend of the 'wayfaring men' in their own homes. Dr. Stalker says, 'Not once nor twice has the religion of Christ, when driven out of the Church, which had been turned by faithless ministers and worldly members into a synagogue of Satan, found an asylum in the home.' Here the follower of Wyclif found his strength. Family religion was involved in that greater freedom from priest control for which the Lollard stood. Wyclif had a tract to his people in their homes 'of this may wedded men and wifes know how thei owen lyve togedir and teche thier children Goddis Lawe.' The Lollard 'society' was a wider expression of this family religion. Their unity impressed contemporaries, and the orthodox chronicler Knighton gives it well : 'unum modum

statim loquelae et formam concordem suae doctrinae mira-
biliter habuerunt.' The official mandates against the sect
speak constantly of ' conventicles and confederacies,' and
the political songs of the period show how prone the
Lollards were to gather together for mutual comfort in the
goodness of their Way, or for mutual resistance to authority.

The prominence of the home and of the society amongst
the Lollards implies that they had discovered the importance
of the ' lay agent.' To the orthodox he was anathema as
' laicus Lollardus,' and a glance at the list of suspect ' confederacies ' will show the prominence of the layman.
One Taylleur at Nottingham has to promise ' never more
to maintain and teach ' Lollard doctrines. The Leicestershire Lollards also bearing the names of their trades are
condemned for ' sowing the heresies ' in the country round.
A list of forty-two names suspect at Northampton show
Draper, Warriner, Taylour, and Couper amongst their
number, whilst the Mayor was their notorious leader, who
' hath made the whole toune in manner to become Lollardes
so that the whole toune is gouerned by them.' Wyclif
had condemned an exclusive priesthood ' who would fain
that all Goddis Lawe were hanging on them for to supply
the people,' and the people of England were to hear for their
comfort ' who is in most charity is best heard of God be he
shepherd or layman or in the Church or in the field.' The
' lanterne of lyghtte ' had passed from the custody of the
priest, and religion came forth from the sanctuary and
mingled with the hubbub of everyday business in market-
place and fair. It found its disciples in the open field and
in the streets of the city, and spoke of a very real Presence,
' When the shepherd on the moor names the name of God.'
In the language of Wyclif, ' a Pater Noster is medeful under
the cope of heaven—for whoso liveth best he prayeth best.'
There was a new reality and a new vigour about it all—

an open-air swing and a new freedom.   John Wesley by
his field preaching won the masses of England to a new
reality of sin and salvation, and it was emphatically to the
masses that the Lollard appealed—to ' sinners, lay persons,
and simple souls.'   It is interesting to notice how this first
' dissent ' gripped the lower classes, for it has been a
lasting characteristic of dissent that it appeals to the man in
the street.   Along with this class-cleavage goes the difference
in political thought which is traceable to-day as in the fourteenth century.   The political and religious opinions of the
Lollard became confused or rather were mutually responsible
for one another.   It was a time when the people were
beginning to come to their own, the spirit of democracy
was abroad, and the capitalist and landowner might tremble.
The Peasants' Revolt was typical of the new spirit.   ' Freedom and 4d. an acre ' was the cry, translatable in the twentieth
century by many words but with much the same meaning at
the back of it.   To such champions of social freedom the
new religious freedom appealed irresistibly, for the peasant
had a way of linking on the spiritual to his prosaic earthly
needs.   Here is his song as he marches on London :

> John the Miller hath yground small, small, small.
> The King's Son of heaven shall pay for all.

Wyclif and his followers were only very indirectly
responsible for any share in the Peasants' Rising, but it is
significant that all the chroniclers charge the Lollards with
complicity.   The town of Northampton is particularly
interesting in the way it has sustained its character for
dissent and liberal politics.   In Richard II's day it was a
Lollard town, and the bishop's commissioners could be
safely defied by an independent mayor, whilst ' Tailours '
formed the opposition.   In Chartist times the same trade is
prominent at Northampton, which is a Chartist town, whilst

to-day it remains Nonconformist in creed and Liberal in politics. The Lollards of the fourteenth century were the humble progenitors of no unworthy succession.

The importance which the Lollards attached to preaching went hand in hand with this appeal to the people. The name flung at them by the crowd, if it be derived from the old German lollen, lullen, to hum or whine, betokened their gift of speech. At least they were famous for their talking powers, and annoyed the orthodox accordingly, as ' Knighton ' writes them down ' valide in verbis—in garulis fortes,' or Gower in his *Confessio Amantis* :

> Nought holy, though thei feigne and blowe
> Her Lollardy in mennes ere.

Indignation against the false, the degenerate Friar, the worldly prelate, made the Lollard sermon in great part, and the whole rang with a constant refrain ' the knowynge of Goddis Law.' That phrase looks out from almost every page of Wyclif's sermons and tracts, and it formed the culmination of every sermon to which the Leicester folk listened, as ' Knighton ' complains, ' Talem enim habebant terminum in omnibus suis dictis semper praetendendo legem Dei, Goddis Lawe.' The Lollard preachers seem to have discovered the art of holding their congregations. Bishop Brunton of Rochester used telling illustration and declaimed against those ' dumb dogs ' of bishops, but he complains of the lack of response to his preaching and deplores the success of those ' extraordinary teachers skilled in tickling the ears of the people.' Another un-solicited testimonial to the interest of the Lollard sermon is found in the statute against them—' they stir and incite ' the people.

Wyclif had done something to train his preachers and give them sermon outlines. His sermons on the Gospel for the Day have notes of instruction at the end. After the discourse on the Rich Man and Lazarus we read : ' In this Gospel may priests tell of false pride of rich men and of lustful life of mighty men of this world, and of long pains of hell and joyful bliss of heaven, and thus lengthen their sermon as the time asks.' It is possible to find an echo of these sermons in the discourses of Wyclif's followers. The Leicestershire chronicler who heard Aston and Purvey preach and entered some of their remarks in his chronicle, has Wyclif's ' Whoso liveth best he prayeth best ' turned into the counterpart in Latin. Whilst we find trace that Aston must have availed himself of Wyclif's sermon for Palm Sunday, for when he preached on that Sunday at Leicester, the master's phrase ' the pain of Christ's Passion passed all other,' is echoed in the disciple's ' Quod poena Christi quam sustinerit in passione fuit major quam tota poena inferni,' recorded by Knighton.

But the individual Lollard added the local colour for himself and filled up with emotion what he lacked in matter. It was the enthusiasm that told, that power to stir those who ' leggen riht hevy as led,' and to make even such exclaim, ' a verie profett speaking with the tongue of an angell.' The Lollard felt his responsibility, he did not spare himself in his sermons; he preached to convince and adopted popular methods. Above all he had the sympathy of the labouring man, and was ' right homely ' with the poor. The sermons read heavily—there is a weary iteration of Scribes and Pharisees in the garb of monks and Friars, and the interpretation of the most living parables is crude. The inn and the two pennies in the story of the Good Samaritan must all be pressed into the service. But that was not how the sermons went in the village church or the Leicestershire lane of fourteenth-century England. The Friar was a real figure then, and the Lollard did not refrain from the personal name—he could be merry at the expense of these 'false prechours' with their inevitable 'collection' and the reflection 'that all this private religion makes not such a legion of saints in Heaven.' The well-fed, idle monk, with the empty 'blabber of the lyppes,' would be another fruitful butt to those who were near neighbours to very real monastery walls.

The Bishop of Norwich's crusade would provide material for another successful topical hit and for ridicule which might explode the once solemn indulgence, as Swynderby says, ' If bulls be the indulgence that men bringen from the court then be they not so much worth as they cost there; for lightlie they might be lost, drenched, brent, or a rat might eaten them—his indulgence then were lost.' But there could be passion too; 'Lord what mirror of meekness is this that bishops and priests, monks and canons and friars, that should be meek and patient and lamb-like among wolves be more proud arrayed in armour and other costs of war and more cruel in their own cause than any other lord or tyrant.' The Lollard knew how to use both the light and the heavy weapon; to make an impression by the mysterious and the awe-ful. The Friar's sermons dealt in fables and marvels; the Lollard thundered in phrases of the Book of the Revelation with the added weight of the Prophets. ' Babylon the great city has fallen '—' Vengeance is mine, I will repay, saith the Lord.' The more gentle appeal was found in the reality of the example of Christ—the prayer in Galilean hills 'a great while before day,' and the preaching in Jerusalem and 'the little upland towns of Cana and Bethfage.' The Lollard was vivid and true—he spoke from experience, and to him the unseen was the real : it was not material pain that made purgatory, even the saints suffer in that cry ' How long ? ' ' And they were bidden abide a while, and that is a pain.' It was no

wonder that there was indignation at prayer to the ' Wyche '
of Walsingham, ' deaf image,' or pilgrimage to the Cross of
the North Door, ' that mere stump of worm-eaten wood.'
Their grasp of the spiritual and the real was the secret of
the Lollard's power. In the struggle of all Church history
between authority and experience they were found amongst
the ' heretics ' who stood for ' the freedom of God's Law.'
It is significant in the wording of the statute against them
in the year 1400 that the sin of erroneous thinking on the
Sacraments and authority of the Church heads the list—
in his recantation the Lollard must promise to be ' buxom
to the laws of Holy Church.' That very obedience would
involve a cessation of the loved preaching, and a poor
' heretic ' on the banks of Wye should give the answer :
' The fishers of God should wash their nets in this river, for
Christ's preachers should cleanly tell of God's Law and not
meddle with man's law, that is troubled water—for
man's law containeth sharp stones and trees by which the net
of God is broken and fishes wenden out to the world.'
The inspiration of the Lollard preacher was personal
religion, his enthusiasm was to save souls ' wending out to
the world.' He chafed at blind authority and the dead
weight of system, and could rise to the real eloquence of
passion in the face of such opposition. It is Palm Sunday,
and there is talk of a Sepulchre with watch and seal, and the
sermon has an application : ' And thus done our high priests.
They dread them that God's Law shall quicken after this,
and they make statutes stable as a stone, and they get grants
of knights to confirm them. And this they mark well with
witness of lords lest that truth of God's Law hid in the
Sepulchre burst out to the knowing of the common people.
O Christ ! Thy Law is hid there—when wilt Thou send
Thine angel to remove the stone and show the Truth to Thy
folk ? ' Altogether too revolutionary—that stone were

surely better left sealed, for ' the weak mind of man cannot comprehend the eternal and exalted God.' So speaks a contemporary poet, pessimistic but orthodox. So men still say who know not of the risen Christ, with His message of grace and sonship for all who believe on His name.

G. ELSIE HARRISON.

V

MILTON'S PROSE WORKS

THE life of Milton divides itself into three periods; it does this more naturally than the most tractable text that ever came to the hand of a conventional preacher. Thus we have (1) the period of scholarship, of early poetry and travel, 1608–1640. Milton was then recalled from Italy by the prospect of civil war at home. He declared that he esteemed it dishonourable to be lingering abroad while his fellow citizens were contending for their liberty. (2) The period of political action and prose writing, which spread over 20 years until the Restoration of 1660. High poetry does not flourish in the atmosphere of fierce controversy. The true laureate of England was lost in the pamphleteer or in the Latin Secretary of the Commonwealth. (3) The closing period of poetry, 1660–1674; the years of *Paradise Lost*, *Paradise Regained*, and *Samson Agonistes*.

Of these three periods, the middle one would seem to offer the least interest. The early poetry of Milton surely reaches the highest levels of classic beauty of which the English language is capable. One of our great critics has said 'It is impossible to conceive that the mechanism of language can be brought to a more exquisite degree of perfection.' Yet the voice of the Puritan reformer is not silent, and breaks out in raucous tones in the very middle of that greatest of elegies, *Lycidas*. Milton went to Cambridge with a view to enter the Church. He discovered during his stay at the University that this was an impossibility. The policy of Archbishop Laud and the mixture of corruption and indifference which was unable to cope with the Romeward tendencies of the leading bishops made Milton a drastic ecclesiastical reformer.

> The hungry sheep look up, and are not fed,
> But, swoln with wind and the rank mist they draw,
> Rot inwardly, and foul contagion spread;
> Besides what the grim wolf with privy paw
> Daily devours apace, and nothing said.
> But that two-handed engine at the door,
> Stands ready to smite once, and smite no more.

Already he is looking to Parliament for reform. One discerns latent possibilities in our great poet which will not allow him permanently to remain in the countryside singing his elegies or his songs of joy and sadness, ' with eager thought warbling his Doric lay.' You are quite prepared to find him in the busy haunts of men and on the battlefield if need be.

> At last he rose, and twitched his mantle blue :
> To-morrow to fresh woods, and pastures new.

Again the pathos and beauty of the third period has in it an appealing power. The strong partisan has apparently suffered shipwreck with his cause. Blind and lonely, in the midst of a world of foes, the principles of liberty and morality for which he contended so fiercely are trampled underfoot. It is natural that his thoughts should turn to that great Israelite patriot whose eyes were put out by the Philistines and who ended his days in glory and tragedy.

Samson Agonistes should be re-read under the new title, *Milton Agonistes*. To get the proper setting for his drama we must live again in the atmosphere of the Restoration. The powerful if somewhat prejudiced words of Macaulay may bring something of it back to us. ' Then came these days,' he says, ' never to be recalled without a blush, the days of servitude without loyalty and sensuality without love, of dwarfish talents and gigantic vices, the paradise of cold hearts and narrow minds, the golden age of the coward, the bigot, and the slave. . . . The Government had just ability enough to deceive and just religion enough to persecute. The principles of liberty were the scoff of every grinning courtier and the Anathema Maranatha of every fawning dean. . . . Crime succeeded to crime, disgrace to disgrace, till the race, accursed of God and man, was a second time driven forth, to wander on the face of the earth, and to be a byword and a shaking of the head to the nations.' Strong words ! the more one knows the history of the Stuarts the more inclined one is to listen to Macaulay. Not all the false sentiment that lies gathered round their name, nor the high chivalry that spent its life-blood in support of them will finally rescue their name as a family from the greatest disesteem due to any in English history.

In his prose works Milton was the spokesman of England against all that the name of Stuart stood for—and a good deal more. He is the first and greatest of our radical thinkers. He is the chief of our political pamphleteers. Not even Swift nor Defoe can equal him. The rhetorical ardour of Edmund Burke is to the glowing periods of Milton :

As moonlight unto sunlight and as water unto wine.

To quote Macaulay again. ' The prose works of Milton abound with passages compared with which the finest declamations of Burke sink into insignificance.' It may seem at first sight that nearly twenty years of the life of England's greatest poet were wasted in these violent controversies over questions which are now forgotten and

deal with personalities which are better buried. Milton
did not think so. He would have set his title to fame
rather on the *Defence of the People of England* than on *Paradise
Lost*. He willingly sacrificed his sight in his great task
of defending the Commonwealth of England against her
many detractors on the continent of Europe. 'When I
was publicly solicited to write a reply to the defence of
the royal cause, when I had to contend with the pressure
of sickness, and with the apprehension of soon losing the
sight of my remaining eye, and when my medical attendant
clearly announced that if I did engage in the work, it
would be irreparably lost, their premonitions caused no
hesitation and inspired no dismay. I would not have
listened to the voice even of Esculapius himself in preference to the suggestions of the heavenly monitor within
my own breast; my resolution was unshaken, though the
alternative was either the loss of my sight, or the desertion
of my duty. . . . But if the choice were necessary, I
would, sir, prefer my blindness to yours; yours is a cloud
spread over the mind, which darkens both the light of
reason and of conscience, mine keeps from my view only
the coloured surfaces of things, while it leaves me at
liberty to contemplate the beauty and stability of virtue
and of truth. . . . There is, as the apostle says, a way to
strength through weakness.'

> So much the rather thou Celestial Light
> Shine inward . . . that I may see and tell
> Of things invisible to mortal sight.

In the Miltonic orations you are at once impressed
with a startling confidence and dogmatism. Milton believed intensely in himself, in his country, and in his cause.
There is no mock modesty about the great poet; he is
well aware that he stands head and shoulders above his
contemporaries. In an age of great classical scholarship

he is the peer of the most learned. Grotius, Salmasius, Casaubon, Bellarmine are but his equals in knowledge. In expression he excels them all. When the war broke out he did not participate in its toils and dangers; he says, 'For since from my youth I was devoted to the pursuits of literature and my mind had always been stronger than my body, I did not court the labours of a camp in which any common person would have been of more value than myself.' His work was to prove that the pen is mightier than the sword. 'Much as I may be surpassed in the powers of eloquence and copiousness of diction by the illustrious writers of antiquity, yet the subject of which I treat was never surpassed in any age in dignity or in interest.'

His passionate defence of the action of the army in the execution of Charles I is of necessity in Latin. It made a profound impression on the mind of the continental peoples, but Milton was too keen a patriot not to love his own language best of all. 'Our English,' as he calls it, 'the language of men ever famous and foremost in the achievement of liberty.' The very name of his country is invariably sufficient to kindle a fire. Perhaps the most famous passage is in the *Areopagitica*. 'Lords and commons of England! consider what nation it is whereof ye are, and whereof ye are the governors; a nation not slow or dull, but of a quick, ingenious, and piercing spirit; acute to invent, subtle and sinewy to discourse, not beneath the reach of any point the highest that human capacity can soar to. . . . Why was this nation chosen before any other, that out of her, as out of Sion, should be proclaimed and sounded forth the first tidings and trumpet of reformation to all Europe? . . . Now once again by all concurrence of signs, God is decreeing to begin some new and great period in His Church, even to the reforming of

F

reformation itself; what does He then but reveal Himself
to His servants, and as His manner is first to His English-
men.' His view of England in those great days was that
idealized picture which has become the most familiar
quotation from his prose works. 'Methinks I see in my
mind a noble and puissant nation rousing herself like a
strong man after sleep and shaking her invincible locks.'
He is thinking of Samson once again, not the poor victim
of Delilah but the saviour of his race and the destroyer of
Philistines. Our modern prophets cannot talk like that,
not merely because they have lost the grand manner, but
because they are so obsessed by Delilah that they forget
the lions that have been ripped asunder and the gates of
Gaza that have been torn down. But Milton believed not
only in himself and his country, he believed absolutely in
his cause. He would never dream that it could be
ultimately defeated. The motto of all his controversial
writings is the same, 'Let truth and falsehood grapple :
who ever knew truth put to the worse in a free and open
encounter ? ' Truth, needless to say, was the cause of
British Radicalism as represented by its most learned
exponent, John Milton.

Mr. G. P. Gooch, in his valuable thesis, *English Democratic
Ideas in the Seventeenth Century*, has demonstrated the importance of this period to all who would go to the origins
of democracy. References to the Roman republic and
the Greek city states are really beside the mark in this
inquiry, except as seventeenth-century classical studies
influenced the formative political thinkers of the day.
What is of interest is that the Reformation of the State
proceeded from attempts to reform the Church and not
vice versa. Laud and the Star-Chamber had more to do
with provoking the Civil War than Hampden's resistance
of ship-money. When Milton, therefore, appeared in the

lists in 1641 with his first pamphlet of *Reformation in England* it was a reformation of the Church of which he was thinking. A year later he appeared in support of the five Puritan preachers who were attacking episcopal prelacy under the transparent pseudonym of Smectymnuus. It may not be transparent to us, but the ecclesiastical world of 1642 soon detected in that grotesque name the initials of Stephen Marshall, Edmund Calamy, Thomas Young Matthew Newcomen, and William Spurstow. In their controversy with Bishop Hall and Archbishop Ussher they had no stouter supporter than Milton. He continued his attacks on prelacy with growing bitterness until in 1659 in his tract on *The likeliest Means to remove Hirelings out of the Church* he attacks the whole idea of a separated order of clergy and would go back to what he regards as apostolic simplicity. It was not in Church government alone that Milton became more radical as he grew older; in theology the same tendency was apparent. Milton as a theologian is much less interesting, however, than Milton as an ecclesiastical reformer, in spite of the profound influence which *Paradise Lost* has had on popular theology. His treatise on Christian doctrine was written in Latin, and did not see the light of day until 1823. It remains the dullest and least inspired of his prose writings, and would be consigned to oblivion but for the name of its author.

It was in 1643 that Milton made his unfortunate marriage with Mary Powell, and the same year he startled the public with his *Doctrine and Discipline of Divorce*. This tract and the others that followed on the same subject bear traces of bitter experience, but the true history of that married life will never be written. He was twice the age of his seventeen-year-old bride, who left him after a month's fellowship not to return until two long years had passed away. Milton's view of the situation is reflected in his writings; it would be helpful to know what she had to say on the subject. Milton's chief weakness is a lack of humour. We find wit and satire in abundance in his declamations, but the humaner note of the humorist who can smile at *himself* is never there. How pathetic is this confession of the stiff and intense Puritan: ' It may yet befall a discreet man to be mistaken in his choice; and we have plenty of examples. The soberest and best governed men are least practised in these affairs; and who knows but that the bashful muteness of a maiden may ofttimes hide all the unliveliness and natural sloth that is really unfit for conversation. Nor is there that freedom of access granted or presumed, as may suffice to a perfect discerning till too late.' Milton's contention was that unsuitability of temper and mental correspondence was a more reasonable ground for divorce than any sin of the body. He does not deign to draw up the scheme for a new divorce bill, but discusses all the Scripture passages on the subject and summons all the authorities to his side that he can muster. With his contentions our present Report on the Divorce Laws would find itself largely in agreement. His great weakness is that in every case the husband is to be the judge. He reveals the strange paradox of regarding the wife as in the highest degree the helpmeet, the mental and spiritual companion of her husband, while holding a thoroughly oriental view of the superiority of the husband in all points of law. He cannot see that the woman could ever have any ground of complaint against a husband who wished for divorce. ' If she consent, wherein is the law to right her ? Or consent not, then it is either just and so deserved; or if unjust, such in all likelihood was the divorcer; and to part from an unjust man is a happiness and no injury to be lamented.' So it would be if all men were cast in the Miltonic mould; but men and women are so illogical and unaccountable. His hypothetical propositions remind us irresistibly of Dogberry's charge to the watch :

' You shall comprehend all vagrom men; you are to bid any man stand in the prince's name.

Watchman : How if a' will not stand ?

Dogberry : Why, then, take no note of him, but let him go; and presently call the rest of the watch together and thank God you are rid of a knave.'

Milton does, however, command our respect by the reverent liberality of his attitude towards the New Testament teaching on the subject. It would have been well if his age could have learned the truth of his great dictum : ' The gospel enjoins no new morality save only the infinite enlargement of charity.' Neither Calvinist nor Arminian could tolerate such dangerous breadth, and his quotations from Protestant divines were all in vain. He provoked the censure of the Westminster Assembly, and was fortunate to escape so lightly; by the orthodox he was never acquitted for what they considered the wild licence of his talk on divorce; the immoralities of the Court of Charles II were trivial in comparison. Milton himself never forgave the Presbyterian divines for their censure. He soon declared his belief that

New Presbyter is but old Priest writ large.

If we sympathize with the man and hear the cry of a wounded heart in his expression about ' a living soul bound to a dead corpse,' we shall find much of permanent value in his writings on this subject without pretending to agree with him in all. It was the next year (1644), however, which was to see the publication of his first classic in prose. ' *Areopagitica :* a speech for the liberty of unlicensed printing, to the Parliament of England,' should be the

vade mecum of all liberal thinkers.   1644 was the critical
year of the Civil War.   A year that witnessed the victory
of Marston Moor and the publication of *Areopagitica*
deserves no mean place in the annals of our country.   It
has been said that the price of liberty is eternal vigilance.
Milton declared that civil liberty could only be assured if
complaints were freely heard, deeply considered, and
speedily reformed.   He proceeded to make known to the
world his complaints against all attempts to muzzle the
Press.   When he speaks of books as not absolutely dead
things, he approaches the humanity of Charles Lamb; in
fact he seems to handle his folios much more tenderly
than he was wont to handle his opponents.   'As good
almost kill a man as kill a good book.'   The cry of battle
is heard in every part of his splendid oration.   'I cannot
praise a fugitive and cloistered virtue, unexercised and
unbreathed, that never sallies forth and seeks her adversary, but slinks out of the race, where that immortal gar-
land is to be run for, not without dust and heat.'   The
key words of Milton's writings are those great trumpet-
calls of humanity, Liberty and Truth.   They have ever
been the chief stock-in-trade of the orator, and by their
very abstraction are for ever begging the question at
issue.   Milton's unquestioned sincerity and elevated idealism saved him from the pitfalls into which a meaner
demagogue would have fallen.   Would this commercial
age listen to his plea that our richest merchandise is truth
or feel the passionate indignation of his appeal : 'Suffer
not these licensing prohibitions to stand at every place
of opportunity, forbidding and disturbing them that
continue seeking, that continue to do our obsequies to
the torn body of our martyred saint (truth).'

The same year he published his *Tractate on Education*,
with its curious disparagement of the Universities.   Milton

is ever the reformer, but he is here looking back to the schools of Greece for his reform rather than forward to Mr. Fisher. There is little to satisfy the democrat in this scheme of academies for 100 or 150 boys, who shall become leaders and generals in the service of their country. There is little doubt that he followed his own counsel for teaching the classics in his own work as a tutor; but the surprising part of the scheme is the emphasis which our great scholar gives to learning the art of war. Our army authorities might be persuaded to consider his suggestion that music should be taught in the 'interim of unsweating' after violent exertion. There is, alas, not one reference to music in the Army Manual of Physical Training.

While Europe trembled with horror at the execution of Charles I, and even the Presbyterians of Scotland declared their disapproval, Milton vindicated the action of the Parliament with characteristic boldness in his *Tenure of Kings and Magistrates*. His appointment as Latin Secretary followed, and he speaks now as a Government official rather than as the learned but eccentric partisan of an extreme party. His first official tract was the *Eikonoclastes* (1650), which was a reply to the popular Εἰκὼν βασιλικὴ of Bishop Gauden, which professed to be the work of the 'martyred king,' and by a mixture of prayers and other pieties captured the sympathies not only of the Stuart adherents, but of many who had supported the Parliament during the Civil War. Milton named his tract after those emperors of Byzantium who 'after long tradition of idolatry in the Church took courage and broke all superstitious images to pieces.' He is very ironical over the claim of the Cavaliers that they represented the gentlemen of England. 'Gentlemen indeed! The ragged infantry of stews and brothels; the spawn and shipwreck of taverns and dicing-houses.' Incidentally he brings out very clearly the fact that the beginning of the struggle found both parties totally unprepared. Milton assumes throughout that the Εἰκὼν was what it purported to be, the production of the late King, though once or twice he hints that he has doubts on that subject. He scored heavily by the discovery that one of the King's prayers was lifted bodily from Sir Philip Sidney's *Arcadia*. The heathen woman Pamela and the most Christian king on the eve of his execution may have had similar aspirations, but it was a most singular coincidence that led them to give exactly the same verbal expression to their emotions. Beyond this Milton says in his most urbane manner, ' With his orisons I meddle not, for he appeals to a high audit.' What does rouse his indignation, however, is the hypocrisy which assumes too intimate a knowledge of the Divine Will and purpose. ' No evil can befall the Parliament or city but he positively interprets it as a judgement upon them for his sake; as if the very manuscript of God's judgements had been delivered to his custody and exposition. But his reading declares it well to be a false copy which he uses and to counterfeit the hand of God is the boldest of all forgery.' There is a violence in Milton's controversial manner which is partly the fault of his time and partly the expression of his own intensity. This alone would prevent him from being considered the model of controversialists or from taking rank in effectiveness with Swift, Burke, Halifax, ' Junius ' or Pascal. His massive learning also sits in places too heavily upon him. When he forgets his spleen and his erudition he often soars in eloquence above them all, but he never achieves the steady clarity of the *Provincial Letters* nor the ironical felicity of *The Tale of a Tub*. The strength and weakness of Milton appear in their completest combination in what he would certainly have regarded as his greatest work, *A Defence of*

the People of England in answer to Salmasius's defence of
the King. It was, perhaps, inevitable in seventeenth-
century controversy that opponents should discover
opprobrious epithets for each other, but we could wish
that our English prophet should have found some better
way. 'You silly loggerhead,' 'slug,' 'most loathsome
beast,' 'vile mercenary foreigner,' 'Burgundian slave,' are
phrases applied to the Leyden professor in the English
translation. There is little to be gained by going back to
the Latin original, for Milton has a unique command of
abusive Latin. He is not content with personal attacks
on the professor, but presses into the home circle with
violent words to Mme. Saumaise : 'a barking she-wolf
at home that domineers over thee most wretchedly.'

These are blemishes in a great argument which power-
fully influenced the Continental mind in favour of the
Commonwealth. It may be that the efficiency of Cromwell's administration of English affairs in their foreign
relations was a stronger argument than Milton's *Defence*,
but that detailed examination of the actions of the Parliament with its mass of parallel instances has a permanent
place among national manifestoes. There is one great
passage in which all Milton's characteristics as a political
writer came out at once. We have there his historical
sense, his passion for liberty and justice, and his profound
belief in his country which had so nobly risen to the
challenge of a present crisis.

'I think I have sufficiently proved what I undertook
by many authorities and written laws; to wit, that since
the commons have by very good right to try the King,
and since they have actually tried him and put him to
death for the mischief he had done both in Church and
State . . . they have done nothing but what was just and
regular . . . according to the laws of the land. And I

cannot upon this occasion but congratulate myself with the honour of having had such ancestors, who founded this government with no less prudence and in as much liberty as the most worthy of the ancient Romans or Grecians ever founded any of theirs; and they must needs, if they have any knowledge of our affairs, rejoice over their posterity, who when they were almost reduced to slavery, yet with so much wisdom and courage vindicated and asserted the state from the unruly government of a king.'

In many of his opinions Milton was in advance of his age; in some of them he was behind it. He had to pay the penalty which original genius so daring and outspoken must ever pay. He bore himself proudly and courageously to the end. As we part with him it shall be in the closing words of his last poem:

His servants He
.   .   .   .   .
With peace and consolation hath dismissed
And calm of mind, all passion spent.

VI

THE TRAGEDY OF OLIVER CROMWELL

THE leaders of the Parliamentary Army held a three-days' prayer meeting at Windsor Castle on April 29 and 30 and May 1, 1648. There was need for prayer. They had defeated the King who had succeeded in seventeen years of misgovernment in alienating the steadiest elements in the national life; the liberties of the subject seemed to be assured. Then, however, the real problems emerged. Months of futile negotiations for a peaceful settlement with a monarch, who still dreamed that he held all the winning cards, had at last convinced them of his complete insincerity. Now, the second Civil War was about to break out in South Wales, Kent, Essex and Lancashire; a Scottish Army 40,000 strong was about to invade England, not as in 1644 to save the Parliament, but to save the King. Worst of all, the victors had fallen out among themselves, and Parliament and Army were at sixes and sevens. It was the crisis of crises in the long struggle, certainly *the* crisis in the career of Cromwell. It had been recognized on all sides in 1646 that it was the military genius of the Lieutenant-General that had been the chief factor in bringing about the royalist defeat. Now, he found himself suspected in all camps. To the Royalists he was the embodiment of the Puritan revolt; to the Parliament he was the most dangerous of the Army leaders who refused to be disbanded; to many of his comrades-in-arms he seemed to be making his own bargain with the King.

His own conscience was clear in that matter. 'I know,' he wrote to a friend, 'God has been above all ill reports and will in his own time vindicate me.' Clouds were gathering in every quarter of the sky. The storm would soon be upon them, and the way was not clear. There was urgent need for prayer.

Such a prayer-meeting is surely unique in English history, and is worth more attention than the historians have given to it. These simple Puritan soldiers believed that they had been led by the divine Providence in all their actions; it was strange that they should be robbed of the fruit of their labours. They had acted, so they believed, in all sincerity, for the good of 'these poor Nations,' but none of the four poor nations in question seemed really grateful. Ireland, Scotland, and Wales were in open revolt, and England only wanted them to go back to their homes. Was it possible that God Himself was dissatisfied with them? They were all ready to humble themselves before the Lord on account of their iniquities, but they needed guidance as to the next step. There was a marked division in their own camp. Some were now ready to take the complete pacifist attitude, 'urging for such a practice the example of our Lord Jesus; who when he had borne an eminent testimony to the pleasure of his Father in an active way, sealed it at last by his sufferings.' Others, however, felt that the whole cause for which they had struggled would suffer defeat if they tamely withdrew now they were confronted by such a mass of problems. It was on the second day, after much praying and prophesying, that the Lieutenant-General spoke. He pressed upon them very earnestly to 'a thorough consideration of our actions as an Army, and of our ways particularly as private Christians : to see if any iniquity could be found in them.' Cromwell was sure that there had been a time when the Lord was with them as an army. Surely it was possible to recover that consciousness now and to be sure that the Lord was again leading His people forth.

It was on the next day, May 1, that the way became clear before them. They saw clearly enough their own wickedness, so that ' none was able hardly to speak a word to each other for bitter weeping.' How is it that no great artist has attempted a picture of this memorable scene? They were the best fighting men in Europe at that time. These were not the tears of fear or of anger, but of repentance and passionate intercession. The divine forgiveness was vouchsafed to them and the way of action was made clear. ' Awake! awake, put on strength, O arm of the Lord,' was the tenor of their intercession, and the reply, as ever, was, ' Awake! awake! stand up, O Jerusalem, put on *thy* strength, O Zion.' Hesitation and doubt were scattered. The decision was unanimous. Cromwell was himself again, for he was at one with his comrades. ' We were led and helped to a clear agreement amongst ourselves, not any dissenting, That it was the duty of our day, with the forces we had, to go out and fight against those potent enemies, which that year in all places appeared against us. With an humble confidence, in the name of the Lord only, that we should destroy them. And we were also enabled then, after serious seeking His face, to come to a very clear and joint resolution, on many grounds at large there debated amongst us, That it was our duty, if ever the Lord brought us back again in peace, to call Charles Stuart, that man of blood, to an account for that blood he had shed, and mischief he had done to his utmost, against the Lord's Cause and People in these poor Nations.' Every word in this statement needs to be carefully pondered if we are to understand Cromwell, to explain the execution of the King and all the effort made afterwards to establish the Commonwealth securely.

Mr. Buchan regards this prayer-meeting as ' politic as well as devotional ' so far as Cromwell was concerned, ' for there he made his peace with the hot-heads,' that is, the extremist levellers and republicans. Mr. Belloc transfers this famous gathering to St. Albans (for some unknown reason), and finds it a very entertaining picture of a revival meeting used by Cromwell for his own ends. Both these writers are in agreement that the old myth of Cromwell's hypocrisy and ambition *is* a myth. He was not a hypocrite and he was not ambitious. Why not believe that Cromwell's cloudy and perturbed spirit was lightened of a great load of uncertainty and indecision at the Windsor prayer-meeting ? It certainly fits in better with all we can discern of his strange personality. In any case, when Mr. Belloc goes on to revive the old legend that Cromwell had been plotting the death of the King for months and that his negotiations with Charles were a sham, he enters the region of complete improbability. A dozen questions arise from that hypothesis making everything unintelligible. We cannot see what Cromwell had to gain by such a tortuous policy, and when we are put off in our inquiries by the statement that Cromwell ' not only excelled in intrigue but excelled in lucidity of thought,' we can only rub our eyes with astonishment and read the sentence over again. He has just been described by Mr. Belloc as the born cavalry leader, he will soon be described as the soldier out of place fumbling ineffectually with futility in his effort to govern. Now he is the master of intrigue and of clear thinking. On the contrary, confusion is the mark of his letters and speeches; rambling and inchoate utterances, much fire and smoke, but the clear flame of genius flashes out only occasionally in some pungent phrase or memorable expression of feeling.   There is a great mind there, undoubtedly, but it is hesitating, meditative and uncertain until in some passionate outbreak of emotion a great decision is registered.   Thenceforward, once action has taken the place of meditation, there is no looking back; he moves with rapid steps towards the goal now clearly discerned.   Gradually he had begun to see that ' the word of a King ' was a broken reed.   His innate conservatism clung to the old constitution of King, Lords and Commons.   Step by step the extremists in the Army drove him on.   As early as November 1647 Harrison was calling for vengeance on Charles Stuart as ' the man of blood.'   It was Cromwell who was the restraining force.   The long strain of exasperating negotiation, the treachery of the man who was trifling with the Army and the Scots at the same time, the outbreak of a new Civil War broke down Cromwell's hesitations. He only needed some clear indication of the Lord's guidance to move forward to decisive action.   He was sure that he had received it at the Windsor prayer-meeting.   In a few short months English and Welsh and Scottish ' rebels ' were scattered and Charles was beyond the reach of any further negotiations.   John Morley is right in his judgement of Cromwell's character when he says : ' he had no stronger feelings in emergency than a dread of forestalling the Lord's dealings.'

Three important books were written on Cromwell in 1934, one of which claims to set forth the truth about his character after dozens of lives have given us nothing but myth.   Earlier lives were ' a mass of slander '; later lives ' a mass of panegyric '; then came Mr. Belloc with the final judgement.   G. M. Trevelyan, in reviewing Mr. Buchan's *Oliver Cromwell* in the *Spectator*, declared that Mr. Buchan's was ' the best book on Cromwell our generation is likely to produce.'   He did not seem to think Mr.

Belloc's *Cromwell* worth so much as a passing mention.
Yet Mr. Belloc's book is well worth reading, as is that of
Mr. F. H. Hayward, which has not attracted so much
attention; they tend to cancel out one another if we are
looking for the real Cromwell, though Mr. Hayward comes
much nearer the mark than Mr. Belloc in his estimate of
the man himself. The moving greatness of the man,
called by an undreamed-of crisis to the battlefield and to
the seat of government, comes out in Mr. Buchan's book
as in none since Carlyle wrote, and we are spared the
extravagances and rhodomontade of Carlyle. Here, also,
we have an adequate treatment of the chief battles of the
Civil War. Cromwell the soldier has never received such
full consideration as in these latest books. The fact that
Colonel Buchan fought in the World War may have given
new zest to his interest, but it is unlikely that we shall
ever have better or clearer accounts than he has given us
of Edgehill, Marston Moor, Naseby and Dunbar. Mr.
Belloc is here a good second. It is a kind of description
in which Mr. Belloc has often excelled, but here he is
beaten on his own field. He is mistaken in suggesting
that Cromwell's real vocation was that of cavalry leader
merely; in that case he would have been found years
earlier serving under Gustavus Adolphus.

' He was a tragic figure,' says Mr. Buchan of Charles I,
' because he was born into times which he could not
understand and to a task that was too hard for him. The
tragedy is there rather than in his death, for his execution
was largely his own blame.' The same may be said, *mutatis
mutandis*, of Cromwell. The forces that were at grips with
each other in a life-and-death struggle in seventeenth-
century England were so nearly equal that a tragic ending
was inevitable for both parties. In the Civil War itself
the genius of Cromwell and the help of the Scots might

lead to the ruin of the King, but that was not the end of the struggle. Against all desire on his part Cromwell was driven to the task of the village constable, as he humorously described it, 'a task that was too hard for him.' Romantic glamour has gathered round the scene of the execution of Charles I, and it may be staged as the last scene in a tragic drama. It is not so easy to write the tragedy of Cromwell, for the catastrophe is not so vivid. The second tragedy is, however, more poignant than the first, by the measure of difference between the greatness of soul of a Cromwell and a Charles Stuart. For those who have never entered into Cromwell's soul, the years of struggle for the salvation of England after 1649 provide merely a comic picture of a clumsy clown struggling to jump a ditch that was too wide for him and floundering back again and again into the mire until finally he disappeared in it altogether. The comic spirit could, of course, read the ineffective career of Charles I in the same way, but a deeper comment on the whole mass of misunderstandings as on some later wars, would have been Othello's heartbreaking cry :

But yet the pity of it, Iago ! O Iago ! the pity of it, Iago.

Great tragedy can only be written of a great personality; at least, there must be some complexity and magnanimity in the soul of the hero if he is to appear on the stage as a tragic figure. This is obscured in popular speech to-day when the miskick of a back, who scores against his own side at football, is described as a tragic mistake and every road accident is a tragedy. If *The Tale of Two Cities* is presented as a tragedy, it is because Sydney Carton's range of thought and emotion gives him a stature adequate to the theme of tragedy. The little seamstress is his companion in the same journey to the same guillotine, but we find her simple, faithful courage pathetic rather than tragic. So

G

Shakespearean tragedy rises to its heights in *Hamlet* and *Othello*, rather than in *Macbeth* or even *Lear*; indeed, in the latter plays it is the more subtle characters of the women, Lady Macbeth and Cordelia, that provide us with the tragic figures. On any showing, Cromwell stands out as one of the greatest, if not *the* greatest personality in English history. He is as outstanding as Shakespeare, and almost as mysterious. It has been said of him that ' he falls under no accepted category,' he ' sets classification at defiance, and seems to unite in himself every contrary,' ' dominates his generation like some portent of nature, a mystery to his contemporaries and an enigma to his successors.' Yet it is only by the accident of the Civil War that we have heard of him at all.

' I was by birth a gentleman, living neither in any considerable height nor yet in obscurity ' is his own account of himself. Not only could Oliver count seventeen relations by blood or marriage in the personnel of the Long Parliament, but out of the fifty-nine names on the death-warrant of Charles I, no less than ten can be counted as of the Cromwell clan. It is incredible that a sketch of Cromwell should be published in our day which never suggests by one sentence that there was any real grievance to rouse the Commons of England to fight against their King. You cannot understand men like Eliot and Pym and Hampden and Cromwell unless you see that (rightly or wrongly) they imagined that Charles and his servants were threatening certain principles in the life of England that were dearer to them than home and friends and life itself. A tender-hearted and affectionate man, with his affections centred in the domestic circle and in the quiet delights of the countryside; a meditative and deeply religious man, whose thoughts travelled as slowly and circuitously as his own river, the Ouse, there was deep down within him a hidden fire that might blaze out like a volcano. This was his strength as well as his weakness, for the fire that might flash in uncontrollable anger, leading to the greatest mistakes of his career, might also become the driving power to carry him through his great concerns on the battlefield and in the councils of the nation.

Is this picture of the future Protector too idealistic? One may enlarge on the rough horse-play of a rustic kind that breaks out in him at times, and may speak in some scorn of his carelessness in dress and his harsh untuneable voice, but even then the humour and humanity of the man break through all appearances. Where do you find a more moving cry of grief from the domestic circle than his words near the end of his life about a son who had died twenty years before? 'This scripture' (Philippians iv. 11–13) 'did once save my life when my eldest son died, which went as a dagger to my heart, indeed it did.' It is the same man who watches with ceaseless devotion through the summer of 1658 by the bedside of his dearly-loved daughter, Elizabeth. The business of the State and his own mortal illness are alike unregarded in the face of that sorrow. Such a father is cast in no common mould. Though Puritanism in our day is the butt of little minds, and the implacable God before whom Cromwell bowed in reverential awe seems an object of amusement to those who have been brought up in the 'good-fellow' tradition of the Almighty, yet man gained a dignity by that fellowship with the Eternal which is hard to discover in the men of our own day. The Puritan had his deep-seated prejudices. His fathers had not lived through the desperate days of the Wars of Religion in vain. Side by side with the Bible in every Puritan home was Foxe's *Book of Martyrs*. Twenty-seven years before Cromwell was born was the massacre of Saint Bartholomew, in

honour of which Rome was illuminated by order of the
Pope. Twelve years later, William the Silent, the heroic
leader of the Dutch resistance, was assassinated. The
defeat of the Spanish Armada followed in another half-
dozen years. These memories sank deep into the English
mind and must have been the subject of much discourse
in the home at Huntingdon. When Cromwell was nine-
teen years old the Thirty-Years War began, and raged on
until within a few weeks of the execution of Charles I.
The hopes and fears of the Protestants of Europe gathered
round the meteoric career of Gustavus Adolphus when
Cromwell was in his early thirties; many of the leaders in
the English Civil War gained their first experience of
soldiering in his ranks. The Puritan brooded deeply over
these events, and wondered whether the day would ever
come when he might have to take up the sword in defence
of what he regarded as the Protestant liberties of England.

A course at Cambridge University cut short by his
father's death, a period at the Inns of Court to acquire a
smattering of law did not make Cromwell a student of
books. Outside the Bible, which was his chief study,
Raleigh's *History of the World* seems to have been his
favourite. We can understand how he would respond to
the great words with which the *History* closes : ' O eloquent,
just and mighty Death! whom none could advise, thou
hast persuaded; what none have dared, thou hast done;
and whom all the world hath flattered thou only hast
cast out of the world and despised; thou hast drawn
together all the far-stretched greatness, all the pride,
cruelty, and ambition of man, and covered it all over
with these two narrow words, *Hic jacet!* ' From the
peaceful fireside and from the fields of the Fen district,
but with a consciousness of eternal verities in the presence
of which our little lives are lived, Cromwell turned reluc-

tantly to the national controversy. Indignation at the treatment of Eliot, passionate approval of his cousin Hampden's bold fight over Ship Money, election to the Short and Long Parliaments led him inevitably to the heart of the conflict. Having been once called of the Lord to this struggle between light and darkness, he was not the man to turn back. One of our recent writers believes that Cromwell found himself as he scattered the Royalists at the head of his Ironsides; another says : ' Oliver had not found himself—that he was never to do in this world,' and the latter judgement is nearer the truth.

At the age of forty-three, in the chaos of Edgehill, he began his apprenticeship in the art of war. The next year in the Eastern Association he is forging his weapon for the defeat of the King. He was finding ' men of a spirit that is likely to go on as far as gentlemen will go.' His ' lovely company ' of ' honest, sober Christians ' at Grantham, at Gainsborough and at Winceby proved their quality. These were the happiest days of his life, for he was fighting the Lord's battles with a chosen people behind him like another Gideon. Then followed the great triumph of Marston Moor. The Scots had guaranteed the victory, but they brought new problems with them. Moreover, Manchester and his like, though true men, were no Gideonites; so the New Model was formed, and the end came at Naseby. Cromwell was to discover that the end was but a new beginning, and the second act of the tragedy consists in the distracting endeavour to find a peaceful settlement where no peace is possible. We now learn that our enthusiast is a man of tolerance, out of the ordinary in these days of stern fanaticism and unyielding principle. So we come to the Windsor prayer-meeting when, as Morley puts it, ' the curtain was rising for the last, most dubious, most exciting and most memorable act

of the long drama in which Charles had played his leading
and ill-starred part.' It was the last act in the tragedy of
Charles I, but the third in the tragedy of Oliver Cromwell,
when the plot became more entangled than ever and the
chief actor found himself confronted with difficulties
demanding superhuman courage and wisdom.

Now was the opportunity to fashion the godly state, so
fervently and so long desired. But the godly could not
travel forwards without the support of the majority, as
Cromwell knew only too well. 'In the government of
nations,' he said, 'that which is to be looked after is the
affections of the people.' The remaining acts of the
tragedy give the story of that failure, but, as in every
great tragedy, the failure is heroic. The fourth act sees
the Lord-General of the Commonwealth in Ireland and
Scotland and leads up to the 'crowning mercy' of Worcester. It contains some dark pages which can only be
understood if we remember Foxe's *Book of Martyrs* and
the exaggerated stories of the Irish massacre of 1641. 'A
puritan armed with a musket and the Old Testament,
attempting to reconstruct the foundations of a community
mainly Catholic, was sure to end in clumsy failure.' Yet
God was still with him to the final victory, and the weary
warrior would gladly then have withdrawn from pre-
eminence and power. There was, however, no discharge
in that war. The last and most complicated act begins.
Seven years of experiment and endeavour, great concep-
tions of Empire for the three Kingdoms and of Protestant
federations abroad, mixed with hasty and unfortunate
improvisations. Worst of all, the uncertainty arises
whether the Lord *were* still leading His servant or not,
with the final pathetic word, 'I was in grace *once*.' For
those who read human nature aright, Cromwell is seen
at his greatest in these last years of his life.

In the quiet period that followed the battle of Worcester, Cromwell discussed the form of settled Government with the leaders, but could find no guidance.   The remnants of the Long Parliament were content to go on in their dilatory way and even, towards the end, to attempt to perpetuate their existence.   After eighteen months of ruffled patience the fires of wrath blazed out in England's leader, and we get the violent scene of the scattering of the fifty or sixty members who claimed to be ruling the country.   'It's you that have forced me to this,' said Cromwell, 'for I have sought the Lord night and day that He would rather slay me than put me on the doing of this work!'   There is no reason to disbelieve him.   No man goes so far as he who does not know where he is going.   So, at least, he had said on one occasion.   Step by step, the lover of law and order, who disliked to use force in Government, was compelled to throw legality overboard and fall back on force.   His next step was to nominate 150 men who feared God and had fought for the good cause to form his council.   'Surely these men will hit it,' he said.   The record of the Nominated Parliament is far better than is sometimes assumed.   It can be described as the greatest failure in modern history of an attempt to found the State upon the Bible.   Oliver opened its sessions with a speech of lyrical enthusiasm.   'Never such a "people" so "formed" (Isaiah xliii. 21) for such a purpose were thus called before.'   He would have been happier if they had been called by the suffrages of the people, but then the people were not yet fit for such a task.   'Would that all the Lord's people were prophets!'   Still, nearly a hundred and fifty prophets were gathered together, and he was full of hope.   Years afterwards, in looking back at that grievous disappointment, he admitted that he was very simple in such an expectation.   Very soon we find him saying : ' Truly I never needed more help from my Christian friends than now.'

We must hurry through the stages of the Protectorate. He was Lord Protector for life, with a Council of twenty-one members, but he must call a Parliament every three years to sit at least five months. Five months (and five lunar months at that) was all that could be endured of a Parliament that would pull the constitution to pieces again. He could not suffer them to go on. If it were his liberty to walk abroad in the fields, it would not be his wisdom to do so when his house was on fire. He felt himself bound, ' as in my duty to God, and to the People of these Nations . . . to tell you that it is not for the common and public good for you to continue here any longer.' So he was compelled to fall back on military dictatorship and the rule of the Major-Generals. ' Truly I have as before God often thought that I could not tell what my business was, nor what was the place I stood in, save comparing myself to a good constable to keep the peace of the parish.' The Constable of England might believe in a generous toleration, but his under-constables increased his unpopularity everywhere. The Second Protectorate Parliament was full of critics. Yet they would fain have made him King by a vote of 123 to 62. This plunged him into the clouds of great emotion. It was a hard decision, and he took weeks over making up his mind. His enemies have said that it was a struggle between cowardice and ambition. They were wrong, for his ambition was to live under a wood side and keep a flock of sheep, and he only refused what might have been God's challenge to him because his old comrades in arms were so bewildered. He had become old and his health was failing; he feared that secular aims were in danger of stifling the divine leading. Could a child of God fall from grace ? The darkest clouds of all were gathering round him. He saw faction and disunion on every side, and dissolved his last Parliament. 'Let God judge between you and me.' Abroad his power had been everywhere recognized. But what was earthly greatness ? Eloquent death was knocking at the door. The passing of his daughter, Elizabeth, was the knell for his own departure. It seemed a tragic failure at the end, but 'God will be with His people' he said. A generation later the English people accepted a settlement of the stern quarrel, such as Cromwell himself would have approved. The seeming defeat was in reality a victory.

VII

ROMANTICISM IN RELIGIOUS REVIVALS

THE borderland country between Romanticism and Religion may be attractive to the adventurous traveller, but its maps are as vague as those of Africa 150 years ago, and disputes about the frontiers are still going on. Even experienced wanderers in the realms of literature are not sure about the frontiers of Romanticism, and the cartographers of Religion are in notorious disagreement. The word romantic has been defined in many ways at different times—as 'imaginary,' 'having no real existence,' 'fantastic,' 'extravagant' or 'quixotic.' I suppose Fanny Burney's heroine repudiated the idea of being quixotic when she said, 'I am not romantic, I have not the least design of doing good to either of you,' whereas the present-day use of the word in certain popular newspapers signifies the most ordinary sentiments. You read, for instance, a headline about a romantic marriage and find that it refers to the fact that two film stars at Hollywood have entered upon one of the short-lived matrimonial connexions that seem the fashion there. It is clear that we are not in the borderland between Religion and Romanticism at Hollywood. Perhaps it would have been better to speak of Religion and the Romantic Revival rather than Romanticism and the Religious revival, because it is that specific movement in literature in Germany, France and England at the end of the eighteenth and the beginning of the nineteenth century that concerns us, and the word revival as

applied to both Romanticism and Religion gives us the clue
for the labyrinth. Is there any connexion between a new
awakening of the spirit of man as it expresses itself with
enthusiastic ardour in literature and with similar intensity
in religion ? The investigation would be simplified if we
could find individuals in whom the two revivals were both
personified, but these types are not readily found. Neither
Coleridge nor Chateaubriand will meet our need. The
great Romantics like Rousseau or Victor Hugo are not
exactly representative in the sphere of religion, and the
religious leaders like Wesley and Newman cannot be said
to represent a Romantic Revival in literature. There are,
however, many dwellers in the borderland territory, and it
is to them that we must look for guidance.

It is natural that we should turn first of all to the Oxford
Movement. There is a famous passage in Newman's
Apologia in which he reviews his last word as an Anglican
to Anglicans. That last word was spoken in an article in
the *British Critic* for April 1839, on the State of Religious
Parties. It accounts for the Movement ' as a reaction from
the dry and superficial character of the religious teaching
and the literature of the last generation, or century,' and the
need for a deeper philosophy. He then spoke of the
influence of Scott in turning the minds of men to the Middle
Ages, of Coleridge in providing the needed philosophy and,
finally, of Southey and Wordsworth; the one in the realm
of fantastic fiction and the other in that of philosophical
meditation ' addressed themselves to the same high principles and feelings.' The Oxford Movement was not the
work of two or three individuals, but was the product of
many converging forces. It was a ' spirit afloat,' he said,
' the result of causes far deeper than political or other
visible agencies, the spiritual awakening of spiritual wants.'

A recent writer on Anglo-Catholicism has stated that the

Tractarian was no innovator. Originality was the last goal to which he aspired. His object was to restore the old. Above all he wished to restore the consciousness of the Church as a divinely created Institution. He was in violent antagonism to the complacency of the English Church of his own day. Violent is the right adjective to use of such a fiery personality as Hurrell Froude. Beneath the wit of his satire and the fierceness of his contempt for fashionable religion was an insatiable yearning for the ideal and ' a sense of the unsatisfying nature of all things.' Such was the judgement of Samuel Wilberforce, and Dean Church compares him with Pascal in many of his qualities. Both ' placed before themselves,' he says, ' the loftiest and most unselfish objects, the restoration of truth and goodness in the Church, and to that they gave their life and all that they had.' The same enthusiasm, but more disciplined, runs through the longer life of Keble, who was, indeed, the source of Froude's inspiration. The same sense of ' encircling gloom ' that troubles Newman is in Keble's poetry, with the same confidence in the Divine and kindly light that will yet shine through earth-born fogs and vapours. The motto of *The Christian Year* was ' In quietness and confidence shall be your strength.' Dr. Brilioth has described Keble's little book of poetry as ' the nuptials of Romanticism with genuine Anglican poetry.' Is it not truer to say that marriage had already been performed by Wordsworth ? After all, *The Christian Year* is an echo, dying away now into silence, while the authentic sounds of Wordsworth's voice will live as long as the English language survives.

In reaction against the Lutheran view of justification by faith and the easy-going religion of the Church of his day, W. G. Ward makes holiness the chief note of the Church, and real holiness could only be found in hardship, sacrificial

rigour and celibacy. By every way we are thus led back to
the Medieval Church, or rather to an idealized view of it,
and if by Romanticism we mean ' the reproduction in modern
art and literature of the life and thought of the Middle
Ages,' then clearly Hurrell Froude and Keble, Newman
and Ward have some real kinship with the Romantics. I
fancy, however, that we shall not be satisfied with so
narrow a definition. We must inquire why men's thoughts
should turn back to an earlier age with such passionate
longing; such an attitude can only come from an over-
whelming dissatisfaction with the Modern Age. It is this
tremulous and wistful yearning for a better life that impresses
us most in Newman's *Sermons*, and what has been called
' the characteristic Romantic melancholy ' broods over all.
It would be unjust to make that melancholy identical with
what seems to us the false sentimentalism of the *Sorrows of
Werther*, for the sadness that hungers for the unattainable
ideal belongs to another world than that in which Charlotte
and Werther shed their floods of tears. There is a Romanticism that turns away from the depressing nature of the
present to some imaginary world of the past, from a mere
hunger for relief, and if it finds its satisfaction in Gothic
relics and dark forests and fantastic grottoes, we had better
call it Pseudo-Romantic and leave it out of our reckoning.
If, however, its escape is accompanied by an idealism that
is penetrated with spiritual insight, then we enter the sphere
of religion, and true Romanticism is born when religion
allies itself to poetry. Blake's *Songs of Innocence* appeared
in the year of the French Revolution and the *Lyrical Ballads*
nine years later, and these little volumes mark the beginning
of the English Romantic movement.

It does seem that if we are to contrast the dominant
temper of English letters in the eighteenth century with that
of the beginning of the nineteenth century, it will be some

such phrase as ' The Renascence of Wonder ' that we are compelled to use.   A new springtide of poetry was born of some strange quickening of the human spirit.   A more fascinating world was discovered than the prosaic every-day world of politics, business, pleasure and routine.   The poets sought for a new glamour as they looked out of

> . . . magic casements opening on the foam
> Of perilous seas in færy lands forlorn.

Hope and wonder led them on.   They could dream of some new and glad experience of life that led men to believe in the possibility of universal redemption.

> Joys in widest commonalty spread.

Romance is inseparable from a kind of faith in man, a mystical sense of the inherent greatness of his soul and the hope that he is more than mortal.   Even his sufferings are the pledge of his immortality :

> Thy friends are exultations, agonies,
> And love and man's unconquerable mind.

There is some form of religion here ; for the faith in man and man's destiny may best find its assurance in a faith in God whose love for man and interest in man's salvation make the eternal background to the fevered and tragic experiences of this mortal life.   The greatest romantic literature is full of this contrast :

> Life like a dome of many coloured glass
> Stains the white radiance of Eternity
> Until Death tramples it to fragments.

The distinctive Romantic tendency in the Oxford Movement, then, was not merely the return to the Middle Ages, but the attempt to recover a lost ideal of beauty, goodness and truth.

Can it, however, be said that the eighteenth century was so barren of romance ?   Carlyle knew it well enough and says unkindly of it :

> ' The eighteenth century, it is well known, does not figure to me as a lovely one.   To me the eighteenth century has nothing grand in it, except that grand Universal Suicide, named French Revolution, by which it terminated its otherwise most worthless existence with at least one worthy act : setting fire to its old home and self; and going up in flames and volcanic explosions, in a truly memorable and important manner.   A very fit termination, as I thankfully feel for such a Century.'

Carlyle was a Romantic, and in *Sartor Resartus* wrote what has been termed ' the Evangel of Romanticism.'   If he wanted revolutions to liven the dullness of the eighteenth century, he could have found at least three others there— the Agricultural Revolution, the Industrial Revolution and the Evangelical Revival.

It is the relation of the last revolution to Romanticism that I want to consider, for its deep effects on the English life and character have only received tardy recognition.   It is a Frenchman (M. Elie Halévy) who has been the first to show the great significance of this Revival on nineteenth-century England, and Charles Wesley has never yet received his place among the poets.   This may be due to the fact that he is regarded as a mere hymn-writer, which indeed he is, so far as the bulk of his work is concerned.   He is perhaps the greatest of our hymn-writers, and certainly the most prolific. He wrote about 6,500 hymns, and in such a mass there is inevitably a great deal of repetition and much that is commonplace. When his poems are not in the form of hymns they are generally concerned with Biblical subjects. Yet some of them have a lyrical quality which should have secured some recognition in the *Oxford Book of Verse* or the *Golden Treasury*. In the prosaic eighteenth century Charles Wesley is the earliest of the Romantics, yet he is not mentioned in the standard history of eighteenth-century Romanticism. Perhaps this is not surprising, as the author refused to admit Blake since he was not discovered till late in the nineteenth century. Charles Wesley's ' Wrestling Jacob ' is a perfect example of imaginative spiritualizing of a scriptural incident in a truly poetical manner, and is worth a place as representing the best of its kind in any general anthology. Jacob wrestling with the angel is interpreted as the Divine struggle for the salvation of the soul of man. It closes with the song of victory after desperate conflict,

> Lame as I am, I take the prey,
>   Hell, earth and sin with *ease* o'ercome;
> I leap for joy, pursue my way
>   And as a bounding hart fly home
> Through all eternity to prove
> Thy nature and Thy name is Love.

The real contrast to this enthusiasm of gladness is found in the cold moral couplets of Pope's religious poems. Even the most glowing religious poetry of the first half of the eighteenth century is cold in comparison with Charles Wesley, and when the Wesleys used hymns of their contemporaries they were inclined to tune them up to their own more fervent key. One illustration will bring out their characteristic quality. The first verse of Doddridge's hymn on the Resurrection was :

> Ye humble souls, that seek the Lord,
>   Chase all your fears away;
> And bow with *pleasure* down to see
>   The place where Jesus lay.

The Wesleys calmly struck out the word pleasure and wrote
rapture, for it was rapturous joy that they had brought into
eighteenth-century religion.   They were not inclined to
allow other writers to alter their own hymns.   John
Wesley wrote in his preface to his hymn-book :

> ' Many gentlemen have done my brother and me
> (though without naming us) the honour to reprint
> many of our hymns.   Now they are perfectly welcome
> so to do, provided they print them just as they are.
> But I desire they would not attempt to mend them;
> for really they are not able.   None of them is able to
> mend either the sense or the verse.'

Whether you define Romanticism with Watts-Dunton as
' the Renascence of wonder ' or with Brunetière as ' the
emancipation of the ego,' Charles Wesley will count as one
of the pioneers of English Romanticism, and the twelve
volumes of the poetical works of J. and C. Wesley are full
of illustrations to prove this.   It is true that they do not
reproduce the thought and life of the Middle Ages ; Charles
Wesley and his brother went further back.   Their whole
aim was to recover primitive Christianity.   The Church of
the first century in their view corresponds neither with the
glimpses we get of the Church of Corinth in St. Paul's
letters, nor with the seven Churches of Asia as we see them
in the early chapters of The Apocalypse.   Theirs was an
idealized vision of the Primitive Church as the Middle Ages
were idealized by Scott and his imitators.   They saw in the
early Church a perfect fellowship of souls in whom the love
of God and the love of man reached the fairest expression :

> Meek, simple followers of the Lamb,
> They lived, and spake and thought the same !
> Broke the commemorative bread,
> And drank the Spirit of their Head.

H

They went further back to the fellowship of Galilee and made the working men of their own time sharers in that society.   Here is part of a hymn to be sung at work :

> Son of the Carpenter, receive
> This humble work of mine :
>   Worth to my meanest labour give
> By joining it to Thine.
>   Careless through outward cares I go
> From all distraction free :
>   My hands are but engaged below
> My heart is still with Thee.

It is impossible to say how the spirit of the common people was quickened, how the imagination was kindled as these lively hymns were sung up and down the length and breadth of the land.   They were not only sung but studied, for the Hymn-Book became the companion of the Bible as a devotional handbook in thousands of homes.   They were known verbatim as the Psalms and Paraphrases were known in many Scottish homes.   By them men were taken out of the grim world of poverty and struggle to a world of beauty, wonder and joy.   The centre of that world was the Cross of Christ, that paradoxical expression of what is highest in God and man.   The fact that it was a paradox made its appeal the stronger.   The passion of Jesus on the tree was continued in the courts of heaven. So we get not only the violent love of such a verse as :

> O let me kiss Thy bleeding feet,
>   And bathe and wash them with my tears !

but the vivid imagery that represents the ascended Lord in his triumph :

> The dear tokens of His passion
>   Still His dazzling body bears ;
> Cause of endless exultation
>   To His ransomed worshippers :
>   With what rapture
>   Gaze we on those glorious scars !

There is, however, a rapture that loses sight of concrete details altogether :

> The o'erwhelming power of saving grace,
> The sight that veils the seraph's face;
> The speechless awe that dares not move,
> And all the silent heaven of love.

This is not the mere ecstasy of the imaginative poet.   It is a stanza that occurs more than once in the *Lives of the Early Methodist Preachers* to describe their experience.   Thomas Rankin, a Lowland Scotsman, for instance, declares that in a prayer-meeting ' in a moment the power of God so descended upon my soul, that I could pray no more.   It was

> That speechless awe that dares not move,
> And all the silent heaven of love.

I had many times experienced the power of redeeming love, and in such a manner as I scarce knew whether in the body or not.'   The influence of the hymns is found everywhere in the six volumes of these *Lives* that record the careers of forty-one of Wesley's lay helpers.   Perhaps the hymn they quote most frequently of all is Wesley's birthday hymn, and especially the verse :

> In a rapture of joy
> My life I employ
> The God of my life to proclaim ;
> 'Tis worth living for, this,
> To administer bliss
> And salvation in Jesus's name.

The note therefore of rapturous gladness is common in this group of men, for the most part sober, hard-working, well-balanced English types drawn from the lower middle-classes or the working classes of the eighteenth century.   Thirteen belonged to the employer class, all in a small way of business ;

amongst the others were a printer, three weavers, a china factory worker, a mason, a carpenter, a baker, a miner, an agricultural labourer and two private soldiers. I do not claim all these as representatives of Romanticism (which is a literary movement), but I find in them that quickening of the spirit that discovers new worlds of beauty, joy and wonder, which may express itself in some artistic or literary form if its attention is directed that way. These forty-one stand for thousands of common people in the drab rural and provincial life of eighteenth-century England who sang their way in imaginative and enthusiastic hymns into these realms of gold. Nor was the perfect city merely

> Jerusalem the golden,
> With milk and honey blessed.

They believed that it was possible to enter the promised land of perfect love to God and man here and now. All the richest Biblical material was used to express that vision of perfection. For them it was

> A land of corn, and wine, and oil,
> Favoured with God's peculiar smile,
>   With every blessing blessed ;
> There dwells the Lord our Righteousness,
> And keeps His own in perfect peace
>   And everlasting rest.

Of course this dream of a perfect life here and now is not an isolated phenomenon in the eighteenth century. We have the famous characters drawn by Rousseau and Lessing in the Savoyard Vicar and Nathan the Wise respectively. A realist might have given a different account of the proto-types of these ideal characters, but it was something that the eighteenth century should desire some picture of perfection. The sentimental idealism that Rousseau stimulated was ready to dream of an ideal character in the ' noble savage ' as a contrast with the degenerate men and women of the period. The Methodist admitted the degeneration, and painted depraved human nature in darker colours than any representative of the Romantic or Pre-Romantic Movements did, but he went on to assert that God's dream for the worst individual was nothing less than perfection.

> My heart, Thou know'st, can never rest
> Till Thou create my peace;
> Till of my Eden repossessed,
> From every sin I cease.

The *Lives of the Early Methodist Preachers*, written for the most part by themselves, are full of rich material, not only for the student of religion, but for the student of social history. They are seldom mentioned in books on mysticism or the experience of religion. The only careful study of them from the psychologist's standpoint is an essay read by Dr. Caldecott before the Aristotelian Society twenty-five years ago. He was influenced apparently by James's *Varieties of Religious Experience*, and entitled his essay *The Religious Sentiment*. The first life in the series, the autobiography of John Nelson, deserves a place as a religious classic beside Bunyan's *Grace Abounding*. It is written in admirably simple English, full of concrete detail, reflecting the strong manly character of a burly Yorkshire stonemason. He knew the meaning of brutal persecution both for his pacifism in the days of the Young Pretender and for his preaching; he has visions that remind us of St. Perpetua, yet he was the practical man of affairs all the time, and his share in the Revival of Religion according to the *Dictionary of National Biography* was 'second only to that of Wesley.' He was converted by the preaching of John Wesley, and says of that crisis,

' That evening, under Mr. Wesley's sermon, I could

do nothing but weep, and love, and praise God for sending his servant into the fields to show me the way of salvation. All that day I neither ate nor drank anything; for before I found peace, the hand of God was so heavy upon me, that I refused to eat; and after I had found peace, I was so filled with the manna of redeeming love, that I had no need of the bread that perisheth for a season.'

A few years later we find him pressed for a soldier by his enemies and being marched under guard through the streets of York.

' The streets and windows were filled with people, who shouted and huzzaed, as if I had been one that had laid waste the nation. But the Lord made my brow like brass, so that I could look on them as grasshoppers, and pass through the city as if there had been none in it but God and myself.'

The two soldiers, Haime and Staniforth, have given us as vivid an account of the Battle of Fontenoy as we shall find anywhere. Through the whole of that Flanders campaign Haime acted as unofficial chaplain to the troops and gathered as many as 300 members into his society. Although many officers tried to repress him, the Duke of Cumberland was kind and gave him his opportunity. Haime considered that he was fighting against three armies, ' the French army; the wicked English army; and an army of devils.' He survived because his life was lived in another sphere altogether. In the horror of the Fontenoy shambles one wounded and dying soldier said ' I am as happy as I can be out of Paradise,' and Haime in his own consciousness of immunity from danger in the hottest of the fighting was ' as full of joy as he could contain.' In another part of the field Staniforth ' was as composed in my own mind as if I had been hearing a sermon. I neither desired life nor death, but was entirely happy in God.' He had only been converted a few weeks before when he was on sentry duty at that unpleasant hour of the night between midnight and two in the morning. He saw the clouds open and Jesus hanging on the Cross. At that moment words of forgiveness were spoken to him and his soul was filled with unutterable peace.

> ' I loved God and all mankind, and the fear of death and hell vanished away. I was filled with wonder and astonishment. The corporal came at two o'clock to relieve the sentries, but I could not think the time was half gone.'

On another of these men who says ' My heart with a kind, sweet struggle melted into the hands of God,' Dr. Caldecott's comment is, ' This is not a medieval Spaniard, but a Yorkshire clothier of the eighteenth century.' We may, also, observe that neither Haime nor Staniforth was a Spanish mystic, but one came from Shaftesbury and the other from Sheffield, and both were rough fellows who enlisted in an army that was not a school for saints. Haime's account of the great change that came into his life is as memorable as that of Staniforth's.

> ' The next morning, as I was going to water my horse, just as he entered the river, in a moment, I felt the love of God flowing into my soul. Instantly all pain and sorrow fled away.'

Another of these commonplace men describes himself as living ' in the suburbs of heaven ' for days together. After a laborious day of praying and speaking to the people he says, ' I was so filled with the love of God, that I scarcely slept the whole night; and yet I got up in the morning as a giant refreshed with wine.' William Black, who carried the secret of his gladness to Nova Scotia, declared that if he ' looked upon the heavens above, or the earth beneath, both sparkled with their Creator's glory; and all Creation seemed to smile on my soul, and speak its Maker's praise.' Later on he says :

> ' My days did swiftly glide away. I could see, or feel, or taste God in everything. The eating a little bread or the drinking a little water from a brook hath many times filled my soul with wonder at His goodness . . .'

We can therefore understand that John Pritchard is making no conventional remark when he declares that ' my every meal was a kind of sacrament : the food I ate was life to my soul, as well as marrow to my bones.' Nor need we be astonished at the saintly Fletcher of Madeley taking some bread and red wine that had been sent out to him into the open where he was talking with his friends and handing it to them with words that consecrated, ' The body of Our Lord Jesus Christ' and ' the blood of Our Lord Jesus Christ.' James Rogers, who was present, says, ' Such a sacrament I never had before. A sense of the Divine presence rested upon us all; and we were melted into floods of tears.' Tears are frequent in some of the Romantic novelists. Of one of Mrs. Radcliffe's romances it has been said that ' every page is bedewed with the tear of sensibility; the whole volume is damp with it.' But these are strong men not given to crying, and such events are a sign of the strength of the religious sentiment.

It would be possible to glean many striking illustrations of what may be termed a romantic view of life from these volumes. Some expressions might be considered extravagant, and certainly it was the habit of the more cultured classes to frown upon this enthusiasm. In their eyes it was mere illusion, all too reminiscent of the fanatics of the Commonwealth period. We, too, may pause at that word illusion, and wonder to what extent these men were the victims of their own imaginings. The Romanticists tried to revive a medievalism that never had existed on this planet. Some of the greatest poems of the movement are concerned with an unreal world whose greatest charm is its weirdness and improbability. Is the sphere of religion also a sphere to which we escape from reality? These men seem to have discovered reality through their religion. In the words of Dr. Caldecott:

> ' So far as this small group of cases goes the final *stability* of the Religious sentiment is uniformly exhibited. . . . They worked by night and by day for periods of thirty, forty, even fifty years, in circumstances in which encouraging results had frequently but little balance over fierce opposition and bitter disappointments. And after their strenuous labours were concluded by physical decline, many of them lived long evenings of life in gradually diminished service: they all closed in serenity. . . . They were men who were regarded as " enthusiasts " by the grave moralists who filled most of the ministries of the eighteenth century; but it was an enthusiasm which had the quality of lasting.'

It may be said, also, that its influence lasted. The very character of the people was changed, and nineteenth-century English Puritanism was moulded by these forces. It is beyond our power to interpret the impulses of the Spirit of God. ' The wind bloweth where it listeth. Thou hearest the sound thereof but canst not tell whence it cometh or whither it goeth.' Men grow weary of a prosaic age and cry aloud for relief from its dullness and apathy. The cry seems to be answered in a strange freshening of the minds and hearts of men, and life becomes more full of significance, of truth and of beauty. Is it possible that the impulses that stirred the common man of England to newness of life in his religion and made him create schools of eloquence, music and self-government all his own, operated a generation later in the sphere of literary activity and ushered in the Romantic revival?

VIII

ARIEL . . THE SHORTER CATECHIST

Over the grave of the greatest of English men of letters
are the familiar words :

> Good friend, for Jesu's sake forbeare
> To dig the dust enclosed heare.

Nevertheless, the sextons of criticism have gone patiently
to work with spade and mattock, and Mr. Frank Harris at
least believes that he has unearthed the authentic ' dust ' of
Shakespeare. For most of us the Stratford bust will
continue to look down

> As god holding no form of creed,
> But contemplating all.

Whether Falstaff or Hamlet of his creations be the real
Stratford citizen, or whether he be composite,

> A deal of Ariel, just a streak of Puck,
> Much Antony, of Hamlet most of all,

we shall never know. The face remains inscrutable, and
the personality eludes us. Nevertheless, the aphorism of a
later critic is true, ' Literature is autobiography.'

We do not expound that saying in the literal fashion dear
to the heart of Mr. Frank Harris. ' Dark ladies ' walk not
Stratford streets alone, but the highways of that city of
reality, whose walls are jasper and whose gates are pearl,
which every true poet treads day by day. Our best literature
is not a mere transcript from the work-a-day life of the

world, but it *is* a transcript from the real experience of a human spirit.   Every great artist is a realist, but his realism penetrates beyond what the mystic calls the world of seeming to the world of essential life.   No writer of our own time has told his own story in his writings more than R. L. Stevenson has done :   the mere perusal of his *Life* by his cousin will go far to prove that statement.   Yet the Stevenson of *Treasure Island*, of *Kidnapped*, and *David Balfour* is R. L. S. as he would be, the adventurer, 'a leader of irregular cavalry devastating whole valleys,' but not the artist of the sick-bed.   Remembering this, every page he wrote is part of his autobiography.   Few among our English writers are so self-revealing as he :   not Goldsmith, not Carlyle, not even Charles Lamb; and it is the charm of his personality which is ever the secret of his power.

We cannot cry ' Forbeare ! ' however much his friends and executors dig about his bones, for they bring to light nothing we would have kept buried.   The fate of his fellow Scots, Mr. and Mrs. Carlyle, has been less kindly.   Shakespeare's epithet could find no more fitting place than over their graves; but the mischief has been done.   The letters of Stevenson bring out his temporary alienation from his father and the rift in his friendship with Henley, but we cannot find in either case that Stevenson was to blame. The sharp clash of wills between father and son seemed to have been one of those painful necessities of life which may not be shirked; and the gradual severance of the collaborators of *Deacon Brodie* was the natural parting of those brought together by accident who were never kindred spirits.   The reply to Henley, written from Monterey, December 11, 1879, will be remembered by the historian of English letters along with Johnson's proud note to Lord Chesterfield : ' My lord, the notice which you have been pleased to take of my labours, had it been early it had been kind, but it has been delayed till I am indifferent and cannot enjoy it, till I am solitary and cannot impart it, till I am known and do not want it.'   Stevenson's words are :

> ' As for my poor literature, dear Henley, you must expect for a time to find it worse and worse.   Now I am fighting, with both hands, a hard battle, and my work, while it will be as good as I can make it, will probably be worth twopence.   If you despised the *Donkey*, dear boy, you should have told me so at the time, not reserved it for a sudden revelation when I am down in health, wealth, and fortune.'

In these words we have something of the secret of Stevenson's hold on the affection of his countrymen—Saxon as well as Scot.

It is forty years since they buried him high up on the narrow ledge that forms the summit of the Samoan mountain. Lord Morley was nearly twelve years of age when Stevenson was born, and Thomas Hardy was ten.   Even his mother's namesake and his own neighbour in earliest days, A. J. Balfour, was a little fellow of three on his birthday. Yet already we have three library editions of Stevenson's collected works—an honour which has been paid to no other later Victorian writer.

We have no doubt that he would ascribe his own success to the degree of perfection he attained as an *artist* in language; for in this he always took himself seriously.   ' It hurts me,' he says to an intimate friend, ' when neither words nor clauses fall into their places much as it would hurt you to sing when you had a bad cold and your voice deceived you and missed every other note.'   And again, writing to W. E. Henley, he tells what his art means to him : ' An art is a fine fortune, a palace in a park, a band of music, health and physical beauty; all but love—to every worthy practiser.

I sleep upon my art for a pillow; I waken in my art; I am unready for death because I hate to leave it. I love my wife, I do not know how much, nor can, nor shall, until I lose her : but while I can conceive my being widowed, I refuse the offering of life without my art. I *am* not but in my art, it *is* me; I am the body of it merely.' In *Prince Otto* the fifteenth chapter was written seven times, and only the eighth version was allowed to pass. *Jekyll and Hyde*, on the other hand, was written in hot haste, after a severe attack of hæmorrhage of the lungs. The first draft was completed in less than three days. After receiving Mrs. Stevenson's criticism he burnt the whole MS. and began it all over again. He took a month over two chapters of *In the South Seas*; four days over his preface to the *Inland Voyage* (less than . . . one decent page of type); and twenty-one days over twenty-four pages of the *Ebb Tide*. Concerning this last achievement he observes : ' Be it known to this fluent generation that I, R. L. S., in the forty-third year of my age and the twentieth of my professional life, wrote twenty-four pages in twenty-one days, working from six to eleven and again in the afternoon from two to four or so, without fail or interruption. Such are the gifts the gods have endowed us withal : such was the facility of this prolific writer ! ' It was here that the contrast between himself and Scott distressed him. ' What makes me sick,' he wrote to Sidney Colvin, ' is to think of Scott turning out *Guy Mannering* in three weeks. . . . And here am I, my head spinning from only having re-written seven not very difficult pages—and not very good when done. Weakling generation ! It makes me sick of myself, to make such a fash and bobbery of a rotten end of an old nursery yarn, not worth spitting on when done.' Little wonder that he was alarmed at Kipling's copiousness and haste : ' He should shield his fire with both hands and

" draw up all his strength and sweetness in one ball." ' In the South Seas, before the early dawn, his spot of bright light would shine out—the first to awake to labour. And yet he longed for a life of more active physical toil. ' Nothing, *nothing* is so interesting as weeding—and the strange thing that I mark is this. If I go out and make sixpence, bossing my labourers—idiot conscience applauds me : if I sit in the house and make £20—idiot conscience wails over my neglect.' He would have been like William Morris, to whom literature, great though it was, was but an episode in an otherwise strenuous life. ' It is a small age, and I am of it. . . . I ought to have been able to build lighthouses and write *David Balfours* too. . . . We take all these pains and don't do as well as Michael Angelo, or Leonardo, or even Fielding, who was an active magistrate, or Richardson, who was a busy bookseller.'

But it is not the laborious artist for whom we have so great an affection—Flaubert was that, and some of us love him not at all—it is the alluring personality as it peeps out in all the best work he did. It is the *curious blend* of almost French gaiety and vitality with the Scotch Puritanism and its stern sense of duty : the emotional and sentimental always there with the stern repression of the dour Northerner.

> A spirit intense and rare, with trace on trace
> Of passion, impudence, and energy.
> Valiant in velvet, light in ragged luck,
> Most vain, most generous, sternly critical.
> .   .   .   .   .   .
> A deal of Ariel, just a streak of Puck,
> Much Antony, of Hamlet most of all,
> And something of the Shorter Catechist.

Leslie Stephen speaks of his ' invincible boyishness '; and Madame Zametsky said to him, ' Vous êtes tout simplement enfant.' It is really the nature of an unaffected child with its romance and almost delightful egoism mixed with an old strain of Covenanting forbears.   It combined to form a very charming gentleman.   You see most of him in that scene when he visits the leper island of Molokai, known to fame through his own defence of Father Damien.   Two Sisters of Mercy are going out to that sad settlement in what may be a life dedication.

> ' When I found one of the sisters was crying, poor soul, quietly under her veil, I cried a little myself.   I thought it was a sin and a shame she should feel unhappy.   I turned round to her and said something like this, " Ladies, God Himself is here to give you welcome." '

He said it because it was one of his golden rules : ' When you are ashamed to speak, speak up at once.'   They advised him to wear gloves in playing croquet with the leper children, but he declined lest it should remind them of their condition.   There is the perfect gentleman.   It reminds one of Francis of Assisi feeding out of the same bowl as the leper in penitence, because he had let slip a word which implied that there was a difference between them.

What was best in Stevenson came from his Calvinist ancestry and his own unconventional view of Christianity. He indeed passed through a phase of revolt against some of the grim features of Calvinism, and would never probably be regarded as rigidly orthodox, but there was no doubt on which side he came down.   His very style, he says, comes from the Covenanting writers.   He never forgot that he was a grandson of the manse; and he writes to Henley in 1883 : ' I fear I was born a parson ; but I live very near upon the margin, and [speaking of a little tiff between them] too much rigour in these daily things sounds to me like clatter in the kitchen dishes.' In the period of revolt against conventional standards of religion we come across several significant passages. Writing to his mother in 1880 : ' The whole necessary morality is kindness, and it should spring of itself from the one fundamental doctrine, Faith. If you are sure that God in the long run means kindness by you, you should be happy : and if happy, surely you should be kind.' And again to P. G. Hamerton : ' With the passing of years and the decay of strength . . . there grows more and more upon me that belief in the kindness of this scheme of things and the goodness of our veiled God, which is an excellent and pacifying compensation.' To S. R. Crockett he said : ' I am no great kirkgoer for many reasons—and the sermon's one of them and the first prayer's another, but the chief and effectual reason is the stuffiness.' Like other preachers he was restive under the sermons of others; but we shall not forget how enthusiastic he became in his later years over the work of the missionaries in the South Seas, and for many months, in the year before he died, was himself a Sunday-school teacher. Though he was always a preacher, I cannot pass from this subject without a recollection of that conversation with the Plymouth Brother he met in the Cévennes, who asked him in French if he knew the Lord.

' " Yes," . . . pointing upwards, " I know Him : He is the best of acquaintances." The old man said he was delighted. " Hold," he added, striking his bosom, " it makes me happy here." There were a few he went on to tell me, who knew the Lord in these valleys, not many but a few. " Many are called," he quoted, " and few chosen." " My Father," said I, " it is not easy to say who know the Lord; and it is none of our business. Protestants and Catholics and

I

even those who worship stones may know Him and be known by Him : for He has made all." '

The greatest appeal in Stevenson's life lies in its *romantic pathos*—his exile and his long fight for life. It was in November, 1873, that he was examined by Sir Andrew Clark, and ' ordered South ' to ward off phthisis. He fought the losing battle against it for twenty years after that. But his real exile began in 1879 in California, when it seemed the end would really come of starvation if not of bleeding from the lungs. But there he met Mrs. Osbourne and married. Fours years of the Alps and the Riviera were followed by three of lying in bed at Bournemouth; and a year in the United States led to the cruises in the South Seas, where he settled for the last four or five years of his life. It was not in that brave heart to complain, but his soul was still in Scotland.

> Home were no home to me, whither must I wander ?
>   Hunger my driver, I go where I must.
>   .   .   .   .
> Home was home then, my dear, full of kindly faces,
>   Home was home then, my dear, happy for the child.
> Fire and the windows bright glittered on the moorland ;
>   Song, tuneful song, built a palace in the wild.
> Now, when day dawns on the brow of the moorland
>   Lone stands the house, and the chimney-stone is cold.
> Lone let it stand, now the friends are all departed,
>   The kind hearts, the true hearts, that loved the place of old.

It is a pathetic fact that there is no novel in the language which more perfectly expresses the colours and forms of Scottish moorland than *Weir of Hermiston*—that unfinished masterpiece on which he was at work the day of his death. There was no doubt about his love for Scotland, ' I am a Scotchman, touch me and you will find the thistle,' and

making a dictionary for the amusement of Edmund Gosse :
' English, The :—a dull people, incapable of comprehending
the Scotch tongue.   Their history is so intimately connected with that of Scotland that we must refer our readers
to that heading.   Their literature is principally the work of
venal Scots.'   In later years Mr. Gosse wrote to him :
' Since Byron was in Greece, nothing has appealed so much
to the ordinary literary man as that you should be living in
the South Seas.'   Now and again his heart cries out against
it, once to J. M. Barrie : ' It is a singular thing that I
should live here in the South Seas under conditions so new
and so striking, and yet my imagination so continually
inhabit that cold old huddle of grey hills from which we
came.'   Or to his old playmate and fellow lantern-bearer
in the boyish days at Edinburgh : ' O for ten Edinburgh
minutes—sixpence between us and the ever glorious Lothian
road or dear mysterious Leith walk !   But here a sheer
hulk lies poor Tom Bowling.'   But most poignantly of all
in his words about Crockett's dedication of *The Stickit
Minister* to him ' in words that brought the tears to my eyes
every time I looked at them.   " Where about the graves of
the martyrs the whaups are crying.   *His* heart remembers
how."   Ah, by God, it does !   Singular that I should
fulfil the Scots' destiny throughout, and live a voluntary
exile and have my head filled with the blessed beastly place
all the time ! '

But the last word about Stevenson will be concerning his
courage.   His was the brave fighter whose love never failed,
and the great task of happiness was toiled at literally till the
last moment.   He fell dying in the very act of leading his
wife to the verandah of their house laughing and chatting to
remove the strange foreboding which possessed her.   No
man of letters since Dickens added more to the real
enjoyment of his fellows, and yet I think the motto which

would most appropriately express what his life was are the words of an old song—

> But I'll lie down and bleed awhile,
> And then I'll rise and fight again.

His fearlessness was shown in physical danger on many an occasion. Andrew Lang tells how he heard a Frenchman say in a café in Paris that the English were cowards, and he promptly rose and struck him across the face. 'Sir,' said the Gaul, 'you struck me.' 'So it appears,' replied Stevenson, and there the matter ended. He was quite incompetent to fight a duel with either pistol or sword, but he would never have hesitated. One can understand his admiration for the English Admirals in the essay in *Virginibus Puerisque*, or for such men as Gordon, or the great missionary martyr Chalmers. 'I would hardly change with any man of our time, unless perhaps it were Gordon or our friend Chalmers.' His courage was not to be tested on the high seas, or at Khartoum or in the high places of the mission field, but in a sterner way :

> 'Wanted volunteers,' he says,
> 'To do their best for two score years !'

It is noteworthy that almost every one of his published prayers has a plea in it for courage. 'Give us courage and gaiety, and a quiet mind.' 'If there be in front of us any painful duty, strengthen us with the grace of courage.' I think that was the one link which united him to that stricken worshipper of force, W. E. Henley. Stevenson found him in the Edinburgh hospital 'sitting up in bed with his hair and beard all tangled, and talking as cheerfully as if he had been in a king's palace, or the great King's palace of the blue air.'

It was the stern voice of duty that would never let him rest. 'I feel,' he says in 1880, 'as far from having paid humanity my board and lodging as I did six years ago, when I was sick at Mentone.' It was one of his maxims, ' Acts may be forgiven : but not even God can forgive the hanger-back.' Therefore he gives us his life-philosophy in *Aes Triplex*. ' It is better to live and be done with it, than to die daily in the sick-room. By all means begin your folio : even if the doctor does not give you a year, even if he hesitates about a month, make one brave push and see what can be accomplished in a week.'

> Life is worth living, through every part of it
> To the last grain of the corner-stone death.

So when ophthalmia confines him to a darkened-room he wrote by the diminished light. When, after hæmorrhage, his right hand has to be held in a sling, he writes some of his *Child's Garden* with his left hand. When the hæmorrhage has been so bad that he dare not speak, he dictates a novel in the deaf and dumb alphabet. When the worst attack of bleeding from the lungs he ever had (before that which terminated his life) seized him late at night in 1884, unable to speak he made signs to his wife for pencil and paper, and wrote in a neat firm hand, ' Don't be frightened : if this is death, it is an easy one.' A critic of his earlier work attacking the optimism of it said he could never have known much of sorrow or suffering. Stevenson wrote to him privately something of his life, and went on to say : ' The medicine bottles on my chimney and the blood on my handkerchief are accidents : they do not colour my view of life, and I should think myself a trifler and in bad taste if I introduced the world to these unimportant privacies.' It is not till the last eighteen months of his life that we begin to see any signs of weariness, and a desire to see the end of the long battle. It was in September, 1893, that he wrote to George Meredith :

' For fourteen years I have not had a day's real health. I have wakened sick and gone to bed weary; and I have done my work unflinchingly. I have written in bed, and written out of it, written in hæmorrhage, written in sickness, written torn by coughing, written when my head swam for weakness. . . . I am better now, have been rightly speaking since first I came to the Pacific; and still, few are the days when I am not in some physical distress. And the battle goes on—ill or well, is a trifle; so as it goes I was made for a contest, and the Powers have so willed that my battlefield should be this dingy inglorious one of the bed and the physic bottle. At least I have not failed, but I would have preferred a place of trumpetings and the open air over my head.'

But that note of self-pity was very rare with him. He had the greatest distaste for the man who could 'wallow in sentiment naked and unashamed.' Indeed, some have questioned whether he could at all be considered a case for pity. Mr. H. W. Nevinson boldly declares him to have been among the happiest and most fortunate men of letters. Happiness was no pose with him, however seriously he may have taken up the task of it. All who knew him were impressed by his vitality. The function of literature should surely be to enhance for us the value of life, and almost every page of Robert Louis Stevenson is groping after fuller life. Leslie Stephen speaks of his 'pervading vitality' as a sign of genius, and compares him with W. K. Clifford and J. R. Green in different spheres of labour. Mr. Nevinson speaks of the 'keen flame of life' in his work. This somewhat weary generation will welcome any physician who can prescribe life for us.

'Tis life whereof our nerves are scant.

In our quest for the means of existence for the drab multitudes we are passing by Him who made the tremendous claim, ' I am come that they may have life, and that they may have it more abundantly.' Every genuine Christian believes that we may only be finally satisfied at that great centre, where the bread and water of life are given for the asking. Yet we shall hail with gladness every runnel and streamlet that seems to bring the life-giving stream down to us, and we may find forgiveness if in our thirst we at times make a mistake. Stevenson had the power in some degree to transmit life to his readers. Even *Treasure Island* made schoolboys of such different men as Gladstone and Leslie Stephen.

Modern Methodism has known no man who was more alive from core to circumference than Hugh Price Hughes. Some of us who loved the man will never forget the shock of awe that moved us when we opened our newspapers that November day in 1902, and learned that he was dead. It seemed incredible. So must the passing of Stevenson have appeared to those who knew him. In the memory of one at least, the death of that fiery Welshman will always be associated with the glowing and highly coloured close of *Aes Triplex*, then but lately discovered. ' Death has not been suffered to take so much as an illusion from his heart. In the hot-fit of life, a tip-toe on the highest point of being, he passes at a bound on to the other side. The noise of the mallet and chisel is scarcely quenched, the trumpets are hardly done blowing, when trailing with him clouds of glory, this happy-starred, full-blooded spirit shoots into the spiritual land.' The heart of youth will respond to such writing as to the call of a trumpet.

It was as boys he caught us with *Treasure Island* with the fear of John Silver and the blind man Pew. How the *New Arabian Nights* pleasantly disturbed us with that weird story of *The Pavilion on the Links* ! He had not the art of Kipling with the short story, but the spell was real to us then. They tell us he could never paint a woman and as boys little did we care for that, but memory recalls at least two ladies in *Catriona* with whom young David Balfours might fall in love, and there will be a kindly corner in their hearts for the elder Kirstie. Ever the boy grown up he seemed to us, and yet he could write at the mature age of twenty-one : ' When I am a very old and very respectable citizen with white hair and bland manners and a gold watch, I shall hear three crows crowing in my heart as I heard them this morning : I vote for old age and eighty years of retrospect.'

However Henley might have despised the ' Donkey,' Modestine, the somnolent, has become an intimate friend. Sterne's tears over the dead ass are less kindly than Stevenson's brutality to the living one. The contrast between the Sentimental Traveller of the eighteenth century and the Inland Voyager of the nineteenth is provocative of odious comparisons. One who arrived at the probable close of the *Inland Voyage* many years after Stevenson recalls with pleasure how interest was added to the ' Hôtel Le Grand Cerf ' at Pontoise, because he had been there before. It was like arriving at the stations in the progress of Bunyan's pilgrims as they followed in the wake of Christian. Our precursor was no seventeenth-century saint, even the Plymouth brother discovered that ; nevertheless supper in bed after a drenching thunderstorm was the more bearable because so merry a pilgrim was on in front. The charm of that idea was so great that at times two prosaic bicycles would have been willingly exchanged for poor Modestine with all her shortcomings. ' I must follow her incessantly belabouring. A moment's pause in this ignoble toil and she relapsed into her own private gait. I think I never heard of any one in so mean a situation.' Our sympathy would be lost on *both* the wayfarers, even when we came to the most tragic part : ' The sound of my own blows sickened me. Once when I looked at her, she had a faint resemblance to a lady of my acquaintance who formerly loaded me with kindness, and this increased my horror of my cruelty.' ' I remembered having laughed myself when I had seen good men struggling with adversity in the person of a jackass, and the recollection filled me with penitence; that was in my old light days before this trouble came upon me.'

The age needs laughter and kindliness and a good heart, and Stevenson at least had these. Bernard Shaw satirized our follies; Wells, Galsworthy and Arnold Bennett analysed them, but they did not increase our vitality by more than an iota. We go back to the early and late Victorians for that. What is the reason for this strange contrast ? It is largely because our moderns are ' Heretics,' and in the midst of them is a strange new champion of ' Orthodoxy.' As for our ' heretics ' :

> The world turned empty where they trod,
> They took the kindly cross of God
>   And cut it up for wood.

For the time being they may ' hang over us like the sky,' but the secret of life is with the powers that seem to be beaten. The ' heretics '

> Are more tired of victory
>   Than we are tired of shame.

None knew that lesson of the unconquerable Cross more completely than did Stevenson.

> To go for ever and fail and go on again,
>   And to be mauled to the earth and arise :
> And contend for the shade of a word and a thing
>   Not seen with the eyes.

With the half of a broken hope for a pillow at night,
That somehow the right is the right
And the smooth shall bloom from the rough;
Lord, if that were enough.

He was indeed far from being the ideal exponent of the faith. There were whole stretches of the territory of Christianity he never seems to have explored—yet he found the way through to the core of reality, and could bid his fellows sit down and hold festival with him. It is a Barmecide feast to which our modern prophets invite us. Stevenson dared to call the latter part of Zola's *Débâcle* ' the ramblings of a dull man who has forgotten what he has to say—he reminds one of an M.P.' We dare not charge our later teachers with being dull, it would not be true. Their condemnation is greater, they are all M.P.'s. And we remember that Carlyle's final and convincing proof of the personality of the devil to Emerson the sceptic—after the round of slums and gin-palaces had proved ineffective—was a solemn walk down to Westminster, a view of the Commons in session, and the triumphant question, ' Do ye believe in the divil noo ? '

Whatever Stevenson was, he was no M.P. He solved no social problem, and did not depress us with human pettiness. His prayers to some seem too finished a production to be sincere and heartfelt, but we have not so learned him. We would join him in the last he read in the family circle, the one read at his own graveside.

' We beseech Thee, Lord, to behold us with favour, folk of many families and nations, gathered together in the peace of this roof : weak men and women subsisting under the covert of Thy patience.

Be patient still : suffer us yet a while longer—with our broken purposes of good, and our idle endeavours against evil—suffer us a while longer to endure, and (if it may be) help us to do better. Bless to us our extraordinary mercies : if the day come when these must be taken, have us play the man under our affliction. Be with our friends, be with ourselves. Go with each of us to rest : if any awake temper to them the dark hours of watching : and when the day returns to us, our sun and comforter, call us up with morning faces and with morning hearts—eager to labour, eager to be happy, if happiness shall be our portion—and if the day be marked by sorrow, strong to endure it.

' We thank Thee and praise Thee : and in the words of Him to whom the day is sacred, close our oblation.'

IX

THE PHILOSOPHY OF D. H. LAWRENCE

D. H. LAWRENCE is the most romantic figure in English literary life since the Brontës. The Nottinghamshire miner's son who struggled up with a scholarship and a pupil-teacher's exhibition to the High School and University College of his county-town to become an elementary school teacher and then a novelist, essayist, poet and artist who not only lived in all parts of the world, but achieved world-wide renown before he died of consumption at the age of forty-four, is certainly a personality of outstanding interest. To the circle of his admirers he is much more than this : he is the Jesus of our day; a prophet and much more than a prophet. The comparison startles a devout Christian by its profound irreverence, but it is an indication of the quality of the religion of the modern man that this comparison should be made again and again by our present-day teachers. Lawrence is ' the man of sorrows,' ' one of the greatest lovers the world has known.' He is himself responsible for this fantastic comparison, for it is clearly in his own mind in his latest writing.

The unimaginative man who takes the joys and sorrows of life as they come with as much courage and faith as he can muster finds it difficult to see where the crucifixion of Lawrence comes in. It is true that he had to fight for health; that is a common lot. Sensitive literary men like R. L. Stevenson have fought a longer battle and the note of self-pity has seldom been heard from them. It is true that

Lawrence suffered during the war, but a soldier who knew the meaning of Flanders to the fighting man may be excused for a certain lack of sympathy with a non-combatant whose chief sufferings seem due to the fact that he had to undergo the crude medical examination that millions of other men endured, and that his behaviour with his German wife near the Cornish coast aroused a certain amount of suspicion. The tragedy of the war affected all sensitive spirits, and there is no indication in the writings of Lawrence that it was more of a Gethsemane to him than to others. Finally, he did suffer from the censor who suppressed poems, novels and pictures, but some men would have regarded these attentions as an excellent advertisement. A censorship is always undesirable, but Lawrence seems to have been a good candidate for censorship, if such control of publications is functioning at all. These are the views of the unimaginative man; he is therefore bewildered at all this screeching about the crucifixion of Lawrence. Perhaps the man was self-tortured and haunted by a persecution mania. Here the unimaginative man is getting near the truth, and may well be sorry for a perfectly honest soul who is more sensitive as well as more imaginative than he is himself. After all, life is a hard business, but we must do our best not to cry too much about it in public.

That the flame of genius burnt in Lawrence there can be no doubt. One who picked up *Sons and Lovers* by accident years ago and was immediately carried to the very scene at Eastwood and turned over page after page as if fascinated will readily admit that. But even in that early book the fatal weakness was there, and the brilliant autobiography that centred in the story of the mother trailed off into futility when his own ineffective sexual adventures followed. So in other books the flashes of penetrating insight and great descriptive powers in picturing scenery and people are frequently choked by dreary philosophy and discussions of the problem of sex, which is supposed by some people to be the ultimate problem of life to-day. The amazing thing is that Lawrence is considered to be specially significant because of his philosophy, whereas in reality what he himself called his 'pseudo-philosophy' bears all over it the marks of spiritual bankruptcy. That may be the reason why so many 'moderns' consider it significant; it is a mark of the chaos of our own mentality.

An alluring advertisement on a copy of *Lady Chatterley's Lover* on a railway-bookstall asked the question 'Was Lawrence a sex-maniac?' This certainly puts the case rather crudely, but his friend Middleton Murry, in discussing this book, says that here 'sex blots out the universe.' 'There is only one purpose in life, and it is the sexual act.' It was one of his last works, and seems to mark the defeat of the spiritual man by the sensual man after years of painful struggle. With whatever fine phrases we may disguise the conflict, the divided self of D. H. Lawrence is that of the seventh chapter of Romans, without St. Paul's word of triumphant deliverance in the last verse. Lawrence was in revolt against the stern morality that read its storm-tossed heart in the words, 'I am carnal, sold under sin. . . . Who shall deliver me from this dead body?' He began with a natural protest against the excessive tendencies of an ascetic Puritanism that regarded the mere mention of sex as dangerous. The spirituality of the Nonconformity in which he was brought up was not strong enough to sweep him away in its exaltant moods. Had the fervent evangelism of the Primitive Methodist lay preachers, of whom he speaks in his book on the Apocalypse, won another convert to the faith, Lawrence had the makings of a prophet of the first order, and the power of the Holy Spirit would have doubtless made him a devotee of the highest quality. As it was, his Holy Ghost became the voice of his own nature. The Holy Ghost might make him want to kill Esau in *The Boy in the Bush* or tell him to go his own way and take two wives if he needs them. Lawrence is sufficiently honest to make the hero's Aunt Matilda criticize this new doctrine of the Holy Spirit by saying, ' You describe exactly the devil driving you.' Yet he had given serious expression to his own belief in these strange declarations.

Mr. Middleton Murry has traced the development of Lawrence's ' disintegration ' with remorseless thoroughness in *Son of Woman*. Yet the remorse is there, after all, for he asks at the end whether he has betrayed Lawrence. Poor Lawrence was always being betrayed, but the chief betrayal of himself came from himself. He not only denied his conscience and the true voice of the Holy Spirit; he set to work to deny love in such a thoroughgoing way that hatred, and especially hatred of women, seemed to be set on a pedestal for worship. What can be made of a modern writer who, having renounced the highest messages of redeeming love, proceeds to search for a new religion in the dark gods of some mysterious past? The more obscure and repellent the old religion seems to be, the more likely is it to yield us the secrets of triumphant living. Now it is the Etruscans, now the South Sea Islanders, now the Aztecs. Their ' dark gods ' may be cruel, bloody, dangerous, but they have the secret of power. This may lead on to a strange glorification of human sacrifice which to the plain man is a mere revival of devil-worship. A Walter Scott may feel the fascination of the banished deities of the Norsemen. His imagination may play round Odin and Thor delightedly and in as harmless a manner as he toys with the dreams of the

Jacobites. His robust sanity would, however, have given short shrift to any proposal to revive the worship of the gods of war and thunder. Lawrence does not seem to know that he is toying with nonsense; he comes back to his dark gods again and again with such earnestness that he persuades us into believing that he wants to shock an age that is full of *ennui* by saying, ' Evil, be thou my good.'

There is a curious anthropomorphism in this worship of the ' dark god,' for that deity seems to be an elongated shadow of the ' hardy, indomitable male ' who fills such an important place in his writings. All that Lawrence was not, but dreamed he might be, if not in this phase of existence then in some resurrection, is the god of his fashioning. His own sensitiveness and tenderness, his sense of futility, his class consciousness must be purged away so that this virile, dominating, aristocratic, ruthless phœnix might arise from the ashes. It is all very pathetic, and out of the perpetual soul-travail it is not surprising that some flashes of beauty and penetrating truth emerge. The truth and beauty may be welcomed, but when we sit down in a prosaic mood to set down what this philosopher is talking about, we have to read it over carefully several times to be sure that we have not set it down in a spirit of malicious prejudice. Then we turn to intimate pages from his life as drawn by admiring women friends and find that they leave us with the impression that the man described by them as ' fastidious, one of the most highly civilized, intellectual men of our day, high strung, abstracted,' behaves at intervals like a neurotic boor. They do not hesitate to describe a series of vulgar scenes and quarrels with his wife, but their admiration for this man, who writes so much in hatred and contempt for women, is not diminished either by his opinions or his behaviour. To them, as to young Maurice Herries in *Vanessa*, Lawrence seems 'a kind of young god, fighting all the hypocrisies, the prejudices, the falsities of mankind, and fighting all alone, his back to the wall.'

Suppose we try to summarize four of his books representing different periods of his work; summarizing in the cold-blooded prosaic manner of a juryman. The *Trespasser* (1912) is the story of a week spent in the Isle of Wight by Siegmund, a musician, with Helena, a devoted admirer. After the manner of Lawrence's heroes, Siegmund disliked his wife and his numerous children (except the youngest) and left them to carry on in a penurious way, while he basked in the sunshine with Helena at Alum Bay or frolicked in the sea with her. He was not a very good swimmer, and barked his shins on the rocks occasionally. This was a real affliction, but otherwise the holiday seemed to be very enjoyable. Of course, he had many psychological problems to discuss, since self-pity asserted itself at intervals. He asked Helena the meaning of ' myself.' ' " Nothing very definite," she said, with a bitter laugh.' She had come of fervent Wesleyan stock and had a hint of a conscience, which scourged her occasionally. Her literary and artistic tastes resented the lower-middle class environment of her home. She liked to quote fragments of Goethe, or Heine, or Francis Thompson, but felt that Thompson must have been ' an ineffectual pale shadow of a person '—something like Siegmund in fact. Yet to her, Siegmund was very wonderful. Francis Thompson had, it is true, something of an intellect, but ' a dispassionate intellect ' to keep Siegmund in order was his greatest lack; so at least a fellow-musician who understood him told him.

In the fields they came across a little Roman Catholic church and were attracted by the crucifix there. The carved Christ with its tenderness and pathos stirred the

K

emotion of Helena's heart. It made her feel so loving and submissive that it helped her to surrender herself fully to Siegmund. When they came across the crucifix again even Siegmund bared his head to it. He felt that he was very like Jesus. ' We are the same; love, the brief ecstasy, and the end.' Siegmund was not so great a figure in world history as Christ, ' yet he derived comfort from the knowledge that life was treating him in the same manner as it had treated the Master.' Those clear eyes did not seem to say anything to him about adultery. Nor did the fact of the sublime courage of Jesus and His complete loyalty to truth suggest a contrast. The week came to an end, but Siegmund's reception by his wife and family was so unhelpful that he hanged himself in his bedroom by means of the strap of his portmanteau. The book closes with a picture of the survivors trying to find some new form of distraction; otherwise, we are where we were at the beginning.

England, my England (1924) consists of a series of short stories written during the war. The story that gives its name to the volume is merely the study of an ineffective man, ineffective as a householder, as a husband, as a father, and as a soldier he is fortunately killed in the war. This is a great relief, but no solution of the problem of the completely fatuous life. There is a complete clash between husband and wife here, and several more occur in the book. In *Samson and Delilah* Samson is a Cornishman home unexpectedly from America after twenty years, who seems to recover his wife after a most violent resistance. Physical violence seems common in these stormy years, as in the story where a crowd of girl 'bus conductors set upon a light-of-love inspector and endeavour (in vain) to make him walk in the strict pathway of monogamy. The women are aggressive in these stories and have to be repelled by ridicule as in *Monkey-nuts*, or gain their ends by accident as in *The Horse-Dealer's Daughter*. In that case, as in *The Blind Man*, physical contact works miracles, but in the former in creating the love of man for woman, and in the latter of a blind man for a possible rival and enemy. *You Touched Me* deals with the same theme, by which an accidental touch awakens unexpectedly desire and leads to family complications involving the submission of a woman to marriage with a man she despises and dislikes. Unpleasant disturbances of married love form the theme of two other stories, while *Wintry Peacock* is based on the love of a wife for a peacock in preference for an unfaithful husband. It might be thought that this constant obsession with domestic infelicity would become monotonous, but the stories are short and there is great variety shown in the character studies, and Lawrence seems more skilful in the management of a short story than in the elaboration of a longer novel. As might be expected, the war is a side-issue in these sketches; a useful element to add confusion to lives that are already well confounded, otherwise of little moment.

In *Aaron's Rod* (June 1922) the opening chapters introduce us to a whole series of husbands and wives and engaged couples at cross purposes with one another. Marriage seems to be regarded as so unstable an institution that public discussions take place as to the most satisfactory scheme by which these ill-assorted couples can play at General Post with each other. Aaron is a checkweighman at a Midland colliery, who also plays well on the flute. We discover later on in the story that the flute represents Aaron's rod that budded; it certainly blossoms out in London opera and in Italian adventures, but it seems more like the rod that turned into serpents, for it has that effect on most of the characters that Aaron has the good

fortune to meet. Indeed, one of the young women who
' seduced ' Aaron after he left his wife and children—
naturally he did leave his wife and children—is almost
represented as a snake. She had a way of licking her lips
with her vibrant tongue, which was reminiscent of the
manner in which the fang of a snake ' flickered.' Aaron's
wife and children get on his nerves in the first chapter,
and though they are all getting ready gaily for the Christmas merry-making in their tidy and well-kept home, Aaron
wanders vaguely off to the public-house and fails to come
back. Strange to say, his wife considers his behaviour
to be rather selfish.

He drifts by accident into the house of one of the local
colliery-owners, who has a married daughter with her
husband, and prospective lover, and also a divorced son
with his fiancée over for Christmas. Later on we discover
that the son has left his wife and children at Paris, and,
when he discovers that his new engagement is rather
unpromising, he crawls back to his wife for a little of the
' love ' which he so sadly needs. Not that he is seriously
thinking of renewing his first marriage vows. He is an
apostle of Socialism and a form of Christianity in which
Christ becomes ' the principle of love.' Like the hero in
the *Beggar's Opera* his aim is to ' sip every flower,' and in
the course of this book he tries to sip a good many. The
author tells us that this alluring gentleman ' spent his time
wavering about and going to various meetings, philandering and weeping.' In order to keep his philandering
instincts alive he needed to eat and drink a great deal, and
his favourite sustenance seems to have been bread and
beer. He gave his stomach ' something to work at ' by
eating half a loaf in his bedroom in the small hours, and
declared that he never got his desirable ' inrushes now,
unless he drank a jolly lot.' He repays the kindness of

his host by punching him in the wind and trying to go off with his wife. This is a peculiarly Lawrentian form of gratitude, for we presently find Aaron acting in the same way, only he mesmerizes the wife of his host with his flute instead of compelling the admiration of the lady of his desire by striking her husband hard beneath the belt.

This philanderer's sister is not so violent in her methods, but her aims are similar. 'She carried on a nervous kind of amour with her lover, based on soul sympathy and emotional excitement.' This is the lady who could not make up her mind whether to follow the 'inrush' of the amour or stay with her husband, and therefore had to put the question to the meeting of her friends, her unfortunate husband being one of the number. She thought he would make an excellent 'lover' for her brother's fiancée. We are left entirely in the dark as to the solution of these complicated problems, but presumably they are marionettes introduced to illustrate the philosophy of D. H. Lawrence. Aaron's wanderings in Italy leave a good many persons of the drama stranded. Unfortunately, the hero himself suffered a sad seduction before he got away from the shores of his native land. It affected him so badly that he felt his 'liver was broken inside' himself, a curious reinforcement of the truth of the Roman conception that the liver is the seat of the emotions. He also got a serious attack of influenza and was nursed back to life by the husband who had been butted in the stomach. They were, therefore, able to compare their views of conjugal fidelity in the period of convalescence and found that they had a remarkable similarity. Indeed, Aaron seems to have discovered his own soul in these revealing conversations, but as he discovered later that his soul had 'gone rotten' the discovery was hardly worth while.

Aaron did make one wild rush back to his wife, but it

only confirmed him in the absurdity of the accepted view of a Christian civilization that women had some 'sacred priority' over men as the source of life and also of culture. In his revolt he would like to forget the words religion and God and love and begin a new mode. Aaron and his interpreter Lilly may succeed in forgetting both God and religion, but they come back to 'love' like moths to a candle; at least Lawrence seems to do so. He is fascinated by women, and always ends by despising them or whining against them. Aaron is left at the end of the book in quite as chaotic a state as he was in the beginning. His friend Lilly tells him that we *must* either love or rule. Women must submit to men, and men must submit to a more heroic soul than themselves; at least that is Aaron's fate. 'And whom shall I submit to?' he asks in the final words. 'Your soul will tell you,' replied the other. However, as his soul had gone rotten his prospects were at least dubious.

St. Maur (May 1925) is the name of a dangerous stallion, the real hero of an unusual story. The clashes of married life having been sufficiently discussed in previous novels, we are now introduced to sexual emotion as kindled by this entrancingly alarming creature. Lou Witt at the age of twenty-five is introduced to us in the first sentence as being completely at sea, in spite of her wealth, success and suitable marriage. She and her husband seemed perfectly mated, but things are not what they seem. She bought St. Maur for him as a present in spite of his disinclination to tackle the animal. The foreboding of tragedy leads us to expect that he will be killed by it; however, when it falls back on him it is only his ankle that is broken, and his wife leaves him in England to be consoled by another fair lady while she departs for Texas with her mother and St. Maur. Her husband and his friends actually thought of shooting St. Maur, but Lou is found with him at the end on a ranch in New Mexico, 8,000 feet up, in isolation from the world. She has not fled to a nunnery because she hates men as men, but because they are not masculine enough.

This odd subject offers ample opportunity for the relation of the soul to Nature, especially to animal nature. Minor characters discuss their reaction to the hidden mystery of life, the Great God Pan. Pan can be seen with the ' third eye ' even in a horse. A Welsh groom and a clever American woman (Lou's mother) in their different ways reveal their fear of Nature and its attraction for them. The groom represents the uneducated superstitious type who believes in ' the other people ' as he calls the fairies; the sophisticated American lady is completely sceptical, but has so much in common with the groom on this subject that she makes a vain attempt to marry him. We are also introduced to another type in a New England religious woman who had to leave the Mexican ranch because of her fear of ' the crude half-created spirit of the place, like some serpent-bird for ever attacking man.' So we leave Lou Witt and St. Maur at the end of the book up in the air and as much lost as she was at the beginning, marriage with the horse being impossible outside the legends of the ancient gods.

Bound up with *St. Maur* is a short story called *The Princess*, which deals with a similar theme. The Princess had a Scottish father and an American mother. As the mother died early, the Princess was left to a father's care, and since he was a trifle mad with an obsession that he was descended from Kings of Scotland, and therefore belonged to a race apart, she lived in an unreal world until his death. She was then thirty-eight, and thought of marriage, but was led by the same fascination of Nature to a similar

Mexican wilderness. Her companion was a wild half-breed who violated her and was shot by unexpected rescuers. She was somewhat disturbed by these happenings, but married an elderly man later ' and seemed pleased.' We are not told whether life ever became a real thing to her or not.

These summaries will sound unfair to lovers of Lawrence, and it may be said that even the greatest works of genius could be made to appear ridiculous by such treatment. It must, however, be remembered that we are not concerned for the moment with Lawrence as an artist. In any case, the form of his novels was clearly of secondary importance, since plot and the dramatic presentation of a story tend to be overlooked in his work. He is really interested in the long-drawn-out conversations such as we find in *Women in Love* on the meaning of life and love and death. He has always something to preach. His sermons are not clearly divided into firstly, secondly and the rest with an introduction and a peroration. He did not even write a preface, after the manner of Bernard Shaw. If we are to find out his aim, it is useful not only to quote occasional illuminating passages from the utterances of his chief characters, but also to see what the general impression of a whole book is. The four summaries given above are genuine attempts to state accurately what it is all about. Always one feels that the author is in dead earnest and also that he is perfectly honest; at least he is doing the best a man can do to reveal the meditations of a disturbed spirit, exploring not only the levels of full consciousness, but the vaguer regions that normally lie just below consciousness. It is all a transcript from life, for with Lawrence literature is autobiography.

His ideal state is one of complete mindlessness, when the uprushes from the subliminal self rule life altogether.

He would be the slave of these true impulses if he could, free from the corrupting play of the intellect. The not-unexpected paradox follows, that the intellect takes its revenge at every point and the mind will demand a hearing, just as the conscience of the spiritual man keeps up its insistent challenge to the sensual man to the very end. Those who think that his so-called philosophy represents the bankruptcy of clear thinking on the meaning of life can only wonder that so many of our intellectuals should give it such unstinted admiration.

D. H. Lawrence was brought up in a Puritan environment and reacted against it with all the violence of an overwrought personality. He embodies the extreme anti-Puritan ideology and is quoted as an oracle in certain advanced circles. So the last sentence of this book may be the same as the first sentence : Puritanism has come in these days (I know not how) to be considered as much a subject for contempt as it was in the days of the Restoration.